Crescendo

A High-Achiever's Journey from Perfection to Freedom

Zen Zeng (PhD)

Ultimate World Publishing
Diamond Creek,
Victoria Australia 3089
www.writeabook.com.au

Dedication

This book is for the people who survived the storm, mopped the floor, and opened the door anyway.

Your strength is real, your resourcefulness impressive, your courage contagious.

Yet, it is your LOVE, for yourself, for life, for those around you, that steals the show.

Take a bow; you have earned the applause, and the quiet cup of tea that follows.

This book is for you. It is for me. It is for my parents, my husband, my children, my adopted family, my larger family, and my inner circle.

It is for the high-achievers, the everyday heroes, and those weathered storms behind a calm facade.

This book is for us.

Contents

"There is a crack in everything,
that's how the light gets in."
- Leonard Cohen

"The privilege of a lifetime is to
become who you truly are."
- Carl Jung

"Life is a symphony: When chaos meets
harmony, every note reveals its meaning."
- Zen Zeng

Chapter 1

The Day
Everything Stopped

I was racing.

From the supermarket to the post office. The bakery to the butcher. Back to the car. Back to the house. Back to the endless list that had become my daily rhythm, my life.

My mind juggled nappies and invoices, dinner and laundry, unread messages and the emotional upheaval of a world on edge. I had to get home to my babies. I had to relieve my husband so he could return to the office. I had to stock the pantry. And I had to anticipate the next need before it cried out.

Then the tyres screeched.

A horn split the air.

A wave of hot wind and metal grazed past me.

I hadn't seen it coming. Not because the car was too fast, but because I was too deep in my own mind to look up.

I looked up now. Saw nothing but a blur... movement, noise, shapes. Nothing made sense.

And then I felt it: the bonnet of a white car brushing my fingertips. The fabric of my pants catching metal and motion. The car had touched me. I had been that close.

Still, I didn't flinch. Didn't gasp. Didn't run.

I kept walking. Mechanically. Blankly.

Because at that moment, I couldn't feel fear. I couldn't feel anything at all. I was numb and lost.

And that was the scariest part.

"Look at her, a stupid woman!"

The voice sliced through the cold air like a blade. Low, sharp, full of disapproval. It struck me like a slap, sending a hot wave of shame through my chest. My eyes couldn't make sense of what I was seeing: everything remained blurred, disjointed, and unreal. But her voice painted the picture for me: an elderly woman frozen on the footpath, eyes wide with disbelief. Not just angry, but dismayed. As if she had witnessed something pathetic and outrageous.

And maybe she had.

The invisible ice inside me began to shatter. Her words crushed something.

Stupid? Me?

But how could that word... *stupid*... possibly apply to me? I was the woman who had graced stages across four continents, who spoke multiple languages fluently, who could navigate complex musical scores and diplomatic conversations with equal skill. I was the one from whom colleagues and leaders sought advice, and the one who could solve problems others couldn't even articulate.

Stupid?

I was the high-achiever, the prize winner, the one who had always been praised for my intelligence, my excellence, my tenacity to overcome any challenges. Teachers had called me exceptional. Peers had called me brilliant. I had built my entire identity around being the opposite of "stupid".

Yet here I was... scattered, distracted, nearly hit by a car because I couldn't focus enough to look where I was walking. I had become exactly the kind of person I would once have judged. How does someone so accomplished, so confident, so intentional, become this lost? How do you go from commanding concert halls and diplomatic stages to stumbling blindly through supermarket car parks?

The word hung in the air, reshaping everything I thought I knew about myself. Not just what others saw in that moment, but who I feared I had become.

I felt lifeless. Irrelevant. And yet... no time to waste.

So I kept walking, slower now, but still moving. Because that's what I did. What I had always done. Keep going, no matter what.

But as I moved, something heavy weighed in my chest. A tangle of feeling misunderstood and wronged, yet somehow guilty too. She didn't see the whole story, of course. This stranger with her sharp judgment... she didn't see the woman holding two children's worlds together with unraveling threads. She didn't see the sleepless nights, the lost income, the fading limelight that once defined my worth. The grief of a concert pianist with no stage. The ache of a mother with no break. The heaviness of a woman trying to hold fragments of a life that weighed more than her limits.

But honestly? I wasn't sure I saw her either: the woman I had become, the one who was falling apart in slow motion. I had subconsciously decided not to see my own unraveling…

I didn't cry. I didn't argue. I just kept walking, slower now. Not because I'd come to my senses, but because I couldn't remember where I was going.

I don't remember finding the car or settling into the driver's seat. I just remember the weight of the metal door as I tried to close it... how even that felt like too much for my body. The groceries had collapsed onto the floor of the car in a heap, much like I did, slumping hollowly into the seat.

Suddenly, I wasn't in a rush anymore. The urgency had drained out of me. The world carried on...

cars moved, people passed, life continued... but something in me had stopped. After months, maybe years of running, I had come to a halt.

Flat, defeated, and paralysed in my own life. As I sat there, the weight of everything that had led to this moment came flooding back...I let the grief take over. My body, my mind, all of it.

At first, my tears fell quietly... hot and burning. Then they gushed. Deep, heaving sobs rose from somewhere deep inside me that had long been dormant. I heard the sorrow, but didn't know who was crying anymore.

Was it the little girl who was never enough... too much, too little, always needing to fit in and rise up? Was it the helpless new mother drowning in expectations, overwhelmed and under-supported? Or was it the accomplished woman I had worked so hard to become, now rendered invisible, irrelevant, reduced in a world that no longer had time or place for her?

It was all of them. All the selves I had carried inside me. And they were all grieving.

I was overwhelmed by self-pity, nostalgia, frustration, shame, terror, and grief. How had I come to this?

I had lost count of the COVID lockdowns, restrictions, stages, and circuit-breakers that Melbourne endured... some of the world's longest and strictest, with months confined to our homes, playgrounds chained shut, travel limited to five kilometres. I understood they were necessary, imposed to save lives. I told myself to be grateful. I tried to make peace with the isolation, to make sense of the loss of human connection. I told myself we needed to survive, stay healthy for now, that my babies would learn to socialise again, that life would return to normal, or something like that.

And when the fullness of 'life' eventually returned, I would figure it out. I would rediscover who I was, or who I was meant to become. The ambition I chose to bury somewhere along the way would be found again. I would feel like me again.

But slumped behind the wheel in that quiet car, I didn't believe myself anymore.

That was the moment I felt the force of something undeniable... the truth I had been pushing down for so long: I had been denying myself the right to feel, to grieve, and to fall apart.

I had forced myself to stay strong, to be grateful and to appear unshaken.

I had met every wave of exhaustion with performance. Every flicker of despair with control. Every loss with a grateful smile.

And now it was all spilling out. Messy, raw, and human.

Maybe some of those tears belonged to a wife, too. To a lover who once believed in the magic of partnership, in shared dreams and whispered promises, who now found herself surrounded by the harshness of everyday living. We were like two ducks on a pond—appearing graceful on the surface while paddling frantically beneath the water, both of us working so hard to keep our small family afloat. My husband was drowning too, in his own way. Working tirelessly to provide, to build, to be the man he thought we needed. We were both performing: him as the steadfast provider, me as the capable mother. But we were performing for survival, not for each other.

We had slipped so naturally into the stereotypical gender roles, into the perfect picture we thought we knew. The successful husband building his empire, the devoted wife managing home and heart. It looked right from the outside. But we had never stopped to ask the question that might have saved us so much exhaustion: Does this actually work for who we truly are?

When had we stopped being partners and become parallel performers, each carrying our own impossible load?

It hurts to admit. But I was no longer crying just as a mother, or daughter, or lost professional. I was crying as a woman whose longing had nowhere to land, and as a wife watching the person she loved also disappearing beneath the weight of everything we thought we had to be.

In the seclusion of my car, I finally allowed time for myself. For the first time in so long, I was willing to stop the internal timer. Running was no longer an option for me anymore... not mentally and not physically. Something in my spirit whispered: *enough*!

Somewhere in the middle of the tears, in that small, suspended moment between collapse and breath, something softened. Not clarity. Not hope. Not yet. Just the tiniest surge of courage to stop pretending. To stop performing resilience. To stop telling myself I was fine.

I didn't know what I needed. I didn't know who I was becoming. But I knew I couldn't go back to who I had been... the woman who had silenced her own exhaustion, ignored her own longing, and measured her worth in productivity and praise.

That knowing, small and quiet as it was, felt like a beginning. Not the beginning of action, but of listening. Of pausing. Of allowing something new to stir beneath the wreckage.

And then, as I sat there in the stillness, something deeper emerged. That near-miss didn't just jolt my body... it had jolted something in my soul. A deep knowing began to surface: something had to change. Not just around me, but within me.

I didn't yet know what that change was. But I knew this: I couldn't keep living like this... fast, numb, and lost.

I had to change. Not for my children. Not for my family. Not for anyone else.

But for me.

I didn't know it then, but that day in the car wasn't just an unraveling.

It was an opening.

Key Moments

- I was moving so fast through life that I stopped looking up, and almost lost myself in the process.

- The word "stupid," thrown at me by a stranger, shattered the identity I had built around being capable, intelligent, and strong.

- I realised how easily achievement and resilience can disguise exhaustion, grief, and invisibility.

- My marriage, like my life, had slipped into performance: two people paddling frantically beneath the surface, but drifting apart.

- Sitting in that car, I finally stopped running. I let myself cry, not as a mother or wife or professional, but as a woman who was unravelling.

- That near-miss was more than a shock to my body, it was a jolt to my soul.

- In the stillness after collapse, I discovered a quiet truth: I couldn't go back to who I had been. Something had to change.

Chapter 2

The Girl Who Could Do Everything

"Anything you set your mind to, you can achieve."

That was the anthem of my childhood. A belief planted early and repeated often by my mother. It wasn't just a motivational phrase. It was the atmosphere I breathed, the rhythm that pulsed beneath everything I did. It became the blueprint of my identity.

Looking back now, I see how that mantra could be called naïve. Misleading, even. Life, after all, has its own rhythm. One that doesn't always follow the beat of our will. Eventually, I would come to the gradual, yet still shocking, realisation: I could not achieve everything I wanted to!

And yet, despite its simplicity (or perhaps because of it), that belief was one of the greatest gifts I was ever given. It wired me with an inner confidence I didn't question, only followed. If there was a challenge, I rose. If there was a dream, I chased. I was the girl who could do everything, and for a long time, I did.

I dreamed big, even as a little girl. Not because someone told me to, but because it felt as natural as breathing. It never occurred to me to think small. I wasn't taught to shrink. I was conditioned to reach and expand.

Much of that came from watching my mother. She was determined to make everything possible for me, determined that I would never be stopped by the same forces that had crushed her own dreams.

The First Yes

At the age of three, I started pleading with my parents for a real piano. The big girl next door had one, and I was mesmerised. Not just by the sound of the instrument, but by her interaction with it. To me, it wasn't a piece of furniture. It was alive. And I wanted to know what it had to say.

But my parents said NO.

It was the 1980s in China. The average monthly income was around ¥30 (approximately the equivalent of $16 Australian dollars). A small upright piano would cost more than a year's salary. Most people were saving frantically for food, shelter, and social security. A piano was, by every measure, a luxury item. An impossibility.

And yet the impossibility stayed with me. So did the hunger to learn.

Fortunately, my family understood what this piano represented. For a family that had once lost everything (education, property, dreams), music wasn't just a luxury. It was a reclamation. My mother's side of the family had once been curious thinkers, highly educated and land-owning. During imperial times, they traced their lineage to poets, politicians, writers, and lords. Even the girls in the family were educated. Rare for her time, my grandmother could read and write with elegance and flair.

That legacy became a liability when the Cultural Revolution began in 1966. Families like mine, with intellectual and land-owning backgrounds, found themselves under intense scrutiny. Our family, once known for its learning and lineage, lost nearly everything. Property was confiscated. Savings disappeared. Books were destroyed. Education was cut off. My grandmother, once respected for her grace and intellect, was subjected to public denunciation rituals known as "pī dòu": public humiliation parades designed to humiliate the symbolic remnants of the old world.

My mother, despite having little formal schooling, was intelligent, dynamic, and fiercely driven. She often jokes now that she was a primary school drop-out. But that joke conceals a deeper truth: She was forbidden from learning. Labelled the child of "bourgeois", "people's enemy", she wasn't just excluded from school. She was told she didn't deserve to know.

But she found her way. She read behind locked doors. She studied from smuggled books. She learned through windows, literally and metaphorically.

She never forgot what it was like to be silenced. So when it came to me, she made a different choice. What they gave me was not their loss, but their hope. Despite everything they had endured, they poured their dreams into me like water into fertile ground. Where they had been told to sit down, they taught me to stand tall. Where they had been denied education, they created abundance for me: the unshakeable belief that I could achieve anything I set my mind to.

And so, against all practical wisdom, they found a way. Despite their initial reluctance, despite the impossible mathematics of it, my parents decided to buy me that piano. They borrowed money from relatives, from colleagues, from anyone willing to lend. It took months of careful negotiation and quiet sacrifice. But they did it. Not because it made financial sense. Not because it was safe. But because denying me felt like repeating history, and they had vowed never to do that.

The piano arrived on a humid afternoon. Neighbours emerged from their homes, drawn by the spectacle. Passersby stopped to stare. I remember their faces: shock, envy, admiration all mixed together. A piano? In our lifetime? For a child? The whispers rippled down the street. My parents were beaming, despite the borrowed money, despite the risk. This wasn't just furniture being delivered. It was a reclamation: deprivation would not be inherited.

Music quickly became the area where I was most recognised. Piano lessons became the heartbeat of our routine, but they came at a cost. Not just time and energy, but real money. Interprovincial trips to find high-profile teachers. Masterclasses.

Competitions. Festivals. While my parents were willing to give everything they had in time and effort, they knew they needed more financial freedom to support this path.

So they made a decision that few dared to make at the time. They quit their stable jobs in state-owned corporations and each started a business. In that conservative economic climate, it was bold. They faced disapproval and criticism, they were scared. But they did it anyway. Not for wealth, but for possibility. They had lived through a time when dreaming was dangerous. Now they would make dreaming possible.

The choice was stark: crush an innocent child's curiosity to avoid financial risk, or take the plunge and refuse to repeat history. Looking at my eager face, my parents saw the answer clearly. Was it safer to say no? Yes. Was it bearable to become the ones who silenced me? No. They had been children of a system that crushed dreams. They would not become thieves of their own daughter's future. This was worth the sacrifice. This was worth the fight.

Learning to Leap

Even before formal musical training began, I was learning lessons about persistence in smaller ways. When I was eight, I still remember being the only one in my class who couldn't skip. A tiny thing, maybe, but at the time, it felt enormous. Everyone else made it look so effortless: the rhythm, the lightness, the flight.

My physical education teacher even told my parents out of frustration that I was not the 'sporty' type.

But I didn't give up.

Every day, before and after school, I circled the oval. Rope in hand. Breath steady. Heart determined. I practised and practised, not out of pressure, but because it felt right. A quiet mission. A way to generate joy for myself.

And one day, I became the skipping champion of the class.

My progress became more than personal. My PE teacher began sharing my story with the whole school. It became an example of what was possible. That no starting point was fixed. That with enough effort and heart, we could go from zero to a hundred.

That moment stayed with me. It was a small victory, but I wore it like a crown. I was eight years old.

Because it meant something. That I could change my reality through rhythm, persistence, and belief. That I didn't need to be born with every skill. I could build them. Step by step. Leap by leap.

Born to Believe

Four years later, when I was eleven, I was accepted into one of the most prestigious music institutions in Shanghai. The school was known for its elite standards, global alumni, and uncompromising expectations. My professors were exceptional musicians, educators, and thought leaders with international careers. Every lesson was a world-opening experience. I wasn't just learning music. I was learning what my grandmother once knew, and later had been denied: how to see, how to think, how to reach.

The depth, breadth, and speed of it all made me feel like I was flying.

And even then, I knew: I was not flying alone.

Growing up, I was often told I was brilliant. Teachers, adults, even strangers would say I was destined for great things. That I possessed a clarity, a sharpness, and a spark. I didn't question them, just as I didn't question my ambition. In my world, talent and potential were currency, and I was born rich.

Their belief became a quiet wind behind me. It validated the hours I spent practising, reading, enquiring, and refining. It made reaching my dreams feel not only possible, but inevitable.

For a long time, I always thought I was born to be different. I didn't know if that belief made me incredibly common (the kind of innocent conviction many children carry) or if it made me strange. But I believed it. Quietly. Unshakably.

When other children complained, gave up, or wandered off when things got hard, I stayed. I asked more questions. I tried again. I stayed with the discomfort. I didn't find these things easy. But I refused to accept that they were impossible.

Everything felt surmountable, if I was willing to invest the time. So I did. I didn't ask whether I was capable, I asked what it would take for me to excel.

And slowly, without realising it, I became conditioned by my own successes (both small and grand). Each one affirming the same truth: I could, and I must.

Failure, if it appeared, was fleeting. Just a sign that more effort was needed. More energy. More time. Other people were allowed to fail, to be human. But how could I?

After all, I was the girl who could do everything she set her mind to.

Reaching Far

Years later, when I applied to some of the most prestigious universities in the world (Oxford, Royal School of Music, Harvard, Columbia, Yale, Juilliard, Curtis, etc.), it was that same quiet determination I followed. I reached far. Not out of arrogance, but out of faith.

And to my amazement, many of those doors opened. Invitations came. Possibilities multiplied. A full scholarship to Western Australian Academy of Performing Arts while I was still in high school. Then a travelling scholarship that carried me to Europe for postgraduate training. Eventually, a return to Australia—to Melbourne, where I completed one of the country's first performance-focused PhD in Music.

It was never about showing off. It was about honouring the path. The one I had started carving all those years ago with a skipping rope and a sense of optimism.

The Silver Spoon Illusion

But somewhere along the way, something shifted.

More and more people began to say I was "born with a silver spoon in my mouth".

And I thought, well, that stacks up. They were probably right. I was born to be different.

On the surface, it made sense. I spoke well. I achieved a lot. I had access to opportunities others didn't. Doors seemed to open easily. I understood how it looked: as if success came naturally. As if I had been handed a life others had to fight for.

But what they didn't see was the rope burning in my hands.

The early mornings around the oval.

The eight-hour daily practice routine at the piano.

The quiet sacrifices my parents made.

The dreams I clung to. Not because they were handed to me, but because I refused to let them go.

What they didn't see was a grandmother who had been publicly humiliated for the crime of being educated. A mother who read by lamplight because she was not 'worthy enough' to grow. Parents who risked everything (stable jobs, social approval, financial security) so their daughter could reach for something that had once been systematically destroyed.

It was easier, I suppose, to believe I had it easy. Easier than acknowledging the invisible labour of hope, grit, and generational determination that got me there.

I didn't correct them. Not at first.

Maybe part of me wanted to believe it, too.

That the ease they saw was proof that I belonged.

And for a long time, reality echoed that belief right back to me.

Key Moments

- *"Anything you set your mind to, you can achieve"*: my mother's teaching became my blueprint.

- My piano dream carried generations of loss and hope.

- My parents' sacrifices turned impossibility into possibility.

- Persistence taught me that effort transforms limits.

- Success conditioned me to believe I must always rise.

- For years, I lived as the girl who could do everything.

Chapter 3

Life Under the Spotlight

The lights dimmed. The intercom crackled: "Ready when you are". My heart caught its rhythm. I was summoned by the exhilarating silence.

Out there, the audience sat in darkness, buzzing with excitement and anticipation. I could picture the glossy black piano, proudly stretching itself beneath the spotlight, waiting for me to reveal its voice. The door opened, I took a deep breath and stepped forward. Applause rose like a wave, and I heard the sharp tap of my high heels against the timber floor.

A moment of exhilaration surged through me. For an instant, it felt like a scene from The Gladiator, when the fighters emerge before the roaring crowd. Only my arena was dressed in velvet seats and chandeliers, my weapon an instrument of wood and steel. And yet, the expectation was the same: to deliver, to triumph, to survive under the gaze of thousands.

I took my bow with grace, the well-rehearsed gesture of respect and authority, acknowledging the audience as though I held the room in the palm of my hand. I claimed my place with authority. I smiled like a winner before I had even played a single note. Yes, I knew this part too well.

This was a routine etched into me since childhood. The bow, the smile, the unshakable stance under the spotlight: it wasn't just performance, it was muscle memory, pride and armour. It was my identity. Before the first note ever sounded, the audience believed they were in the presence of certainty, mastery, and elegance. And I knew how to give them that.

The act began before I even reached the piano. I was in character the moment the first glimpse of my dress caught the eyes of the audience. That was the signal for them, and for me. I was ready. I was on. The performance had already begun, long before my fingers touched the keys.

I was opening the concert with a mammoth piece: Fantasia Bætica by the Spanish composer Manuel de Falla, often regarded as the pinnacle of Spanish piano music, composed by the father of Spanish music himself. It was technical. It was unrelenting. It demanded brilliance and nuance in equal measure. Full of light and shade, rich with musical and cultural inflections. It was the kind of work that left no room for compromise.

And I was not scared. I felt completely alive. My body leaned forward, balanced at the edge of the stool, every nerve sharpened to the tips of my fingers. I captured every shade, every tone, and every colour that piece demanded. My music cried. It triumphed. It howled, protested, and laughed. It was theatre, passion, defiance, poetry, all translated through me.

I felt like a master of puppetry, commanding every phrase, every silence. My movements looked superb, apt, magnificent, at least that's what I intended them to be. The choreography of my body was as much a part of the spectacle as the sound itself. And in that moment, I was in love: with the music, with the precision, with the unrelenting demand it placed on me, and with the precious, fleeting space it gave me to shine.

And then came the next assault. Angular chords, jagged and insistent, tore through the air with a kind of anguish that demanded everything from my full body. Its sound was raw, almost violent, pushing against the edges of beauty. I pressed forward, layering multiple voices, double octaves, crossing hands in a frenzy that felt both chaotic and precise. The textures grew denser, the pedaling rapid-fire, my body straining to hold clarity in the storm.

The crescendo swelled, dramatic and unrelenting, until it felt as though the piano itself might burst open under the weight of it. Fortissimo, then fortississimo. Every sound demanded more, more, more. There was no room to retreat, no chance to catch my breath. I was on the edge, and I needed my audience on the edge of their seats with me, riding that dangerous crest between mastery and collapse.

Thump! The final chord landed with precision and force, ringing out into the hall with both intensity and finality. I lifted my hands from the keys, a triumphant smile already on my face. In one motion I leapt to my feet, looked up, looked around, opened my arms wide to embrace the hall, then bowed deeply to the thunderous applause.

The audience rose to their feet, clapping with gusto, their shouts cutting through the roar: "Brava! More!" The ovation pulsed like a storm, and I smiled as though their accolades were the most natural thing in the world. Proud. Triumphant. In control.

I had given them everything they came for. And on the outside, I looked exactly as they expected: the unshakable performer, beaming in victory, commanding the stage.

I took one more bow, sweeping my gaze across the hall, up to the balconies, down to the front rows, making sure I had acknowledged everyone. Then I gathered my dress in my hands, gracefully, deliberately, and strode off the stage. The applause followed me, fading only reluctantly, a chorus of "Whoa!" "Brava," "More!" echoing as I disappeared into the wings.

Backstage, I was met with more generous, affirming accolades. Someone pressed a bottle of water into my hand. I drank, nodded, kicked off my high heels, and picked them up like a soldier's worn boots after battle. Then I made my way to the mirror, collapsed into the chair, and let out a long, cavernous sigh. My body draped itself heavily, as though it had been waiting for this release all along.

In the silence that followed, something stirred beneath the triumph. A whisper of exhaustion I had learned to ignore. The mask had come off with my shoes, and for just a moment, the loneliness hit me.

As I sat there catching my breath, my mind drifted back to how this day had actually begun. That morning, I had woken to find my bed was soaked with blood—bright, shocking, like something from a medical emergency. I had no idea what was happening to my body. My first instinct was to rationalise: perhaps stress had triggered an unusually heavy cycle before such an important performance. I cleaned up quickly, took some painkillers, and continued with my pre-concert routine as if nothing had happened.

I told no one. It was an ordinary work day: everyone seemed to have disappeared into their daily hustle and bustle, and my husband was on a work trip in a completely different timezone. There was no time, no space, no focus for anything but the performance ahead. I was uncertain about what was wrong, and my mind had to compartmentalise completely.

This was what I had been trained for my entire life. Since I began learning piano at three years old, I had studied under the most elite, toughest, and respected masters across different institutions, cultures, and continents. These were extraordinary musicians, who had achieved the highest levels of excellence in their fields. Despite their varied backgrounds, the message was overwhelmingly the same: nobody cares, just put on a show, and it's got to be good!

That meant to me that the pursuit of perfection required complete dedication, and personal struggles could not interfere with the delivery of excellence. This was how they had been taught, how they had achieved mastery in their own territories, and what had worked for them in building remarkable careers.

I had absorbed this conditioning completely. Only weeks later would I discover it was a serious post-surgical infection that required immediate medical attention. But that night, I performed as though my body wasn't sending distress signals I had trained myself to ignore.

Who could I have told anyway? Who would have understood that beneath all this triumph, I was struggling, bleeding, alone? How much of myself was performance, and how much was... me?

But the thought was fleeting. There were people waiting to congratulate me, a reception to attend, reviews to be written. I straightened my shoulders, slipped my shoes back on, and prepared to be brilliant once again.

Key Moments

- The stage was my arena, applause my proof.

- Performance became armour as much as art.

- Triumph on the outside often hid struggle within.

- I learned to ignore pain, even crisis, in pursuit of perfection.

- The ovation was loud, but backstage, I was alone.

Chapter 4

Backstage: The Hidden Weight of Holding It All Together

Languages, culture, and nuance have always been in my DNA. They opened my eyes and lifted my heart. From a young age, the idea of becoming an interpreter, an interpreter of significant exchanges, felt like a dream. It felt ironic, given my family's history and my parents' constant warnings to stay apolitical.

Perhaps interpreting felt apolitical to me. It was a way to be actively involved in world events, in high-stakes decisions, in moments that shaped history, without ever having to risk a voice of my own.

When we moved countries, one of the hidden gifts was language. Learning English was hard at first, but soon it felt progressive, natural, as if my "musician's ear" instinctively tuned into new rhythms and sounds. People often told me I was lucky, that my musical training gave me agility in languages. I began to believe them.

By the time I reached university, I felt ready to formalise this gift. I was already deeply immersed in music performance, majoring in piano, alongside graduate studies in teaching. This meant I was representing Australia on international stages, performing with world orchestras and recording for the Australian Broadcasting Corporation. My days were consumed with endless lectures, rehearsals, assignments, and hours of practice.

Yet the high-achiever in me decided this was the right moment to take on more: a qualification in interpreting and translating through NAATI, Australia's national standards body for the profession. The accreditation was rigorous, setting international best practices, and highly competitive.

The NAATI administrators made no attempt to soften the pressure. At the time, accreditation in Australia was being reshaped to lead international standards, and expectations were exacting. Getting into the course had been competitive. But in our first week, we were told bluntly that only 30 percent of candidates would pass. I looked around the room at my peers: all older, more seasoned in life and work. I felt a surge of apprehension. What was I doing here, trying to wrangle another qualification on top of an already full plate? And yet the thought of failure was intolerable. I had never failed. If I was going to pour my time and energy into this, I had to pass. I would pass.

So I studied, very hard. I was proud of being in the course, motivated by my love for language and the possibilities it promised. But what stayed with me most was not just the techniques of interpreting, the strategies of simultaneous translation, the agility of switching between languages, but the training in ethics.

Ethics was, in many ways, the hidden curriculum. It wasn't just about words, but about the professional self you had to become. How to handle yourself in high-stakes rooms. How to maintain composure when everything around you was collapsing. How to absorb the moral weight of decisions without interfering. Behind the curtain of words lay a deeper requirement: to be transparent: absorb everything, express nothing.

I still recall vividly the shock I felt in those ethics classes. We were taught to emotionally detach, to draw a strict line between ourselves and the world unfolding around us. No emotions. No reactions. Our job was to create the illusion that speakers of different languages were communicating directly, seamlessly. The interpreter was to be emotionally transparent, as I came to call it. Whatever we absorbed, we were expected to release immediately. No processing, no pause, no trace left behind.

We studied case after case: war crimes, police interrogations, political assassinations, medical emergencies. Even in the face of trauma (unspeakable, dire, unfathomable situations), the command was always the same: interpret faithfully, exactly, and without noise. Never let your own humanity seep through.

Eventually, as I expected of myself, I graduated with flying colours. Almost immediately I was crowned with one of the highest badges interpreters could hold in Australia, and by international standards as well. I was ready to step onto the international stage as a recognised, fully-fledged, professional interpreter of English and Chinese.

And then the theory became reality.

The Invisible Woman

So I started to live my dream. I worked for national interpreting agencies and in-house interpreting departments before starting my own interpreting and translating company. And shortly I found myself moving across an extraordinary range of arenas: the solemn weight of Australian law courts where every word carried legal consequence; the urgency of state hospitals translating between life and death; tourism authorities eager to charm visitors; mining giants negotiating billion-dollar deals; political conferences where rhetoric collided; and eventually the parliament itself, where I served as the personal interpreter for the Speaker of Western Australia.

My assignments carried me into places that could not have been more varied: confidential police operations ending in fully armed raids; vast mining sites where I stood in safety boots and safety hat surrounded by rare earth; private yachts where trade deals were leisurely discussed; emergency rooms where families held their breath; behind closed doors where diplomatic negotiations unfolded beneath the veneer of formal proceedings.

The adrenaline was real. The pride was real. But so was the cost. Because every time I stepped into those spaces, I left myself behind. Whatever tension, anger, grief, or urgency I absorbed had to be released immediately. No time to process, and no room for reflection. I was emotionally transparent, a conduit with no residue.

The better I performed, the less of me there was.

This went for several years, during which I worked as a conference interpreter at the highest levels: in politics, diplomacy, national security, trade, and law enforcement. I was just 24 years old when I found myself in rooms where million-dollar deals were struck, where state secrets were shared, where lives hung in the balance. While my peers were navigating entry-level jobs and weekend parties, I was upholding (if not setting) the utmost high standards in situations that seasoned professionals twice my age would find daunting.

I wore this responsibility like armour. I was, in every way, a consummate professional: fluent, fast, emotionally contained. I prided myself on never faltering, never interfering, never letting anything personal seep through.

But backstage, the silence grew louder.

The Breaking Point

And then came the day when all my training, all the ethics, all the discipline I had lived by, collided with the simple fact of being human.

It began in darkness, at the edge of dawn. High speed, precision exchanges, coded messages, and sharp looks flicking across the shadows. A highly confidential, large-scale police operation was in motion, one that had taken weeks to plan. The atmosphere was electric, taut with urgency, every person moving with practised precision. As one of a small team of interpreters hand-picked for the operation, each covering different languages, I was swept into the centre of it, supporting every stage as the operation unfolded.

When the noise, the action, the adrenaline finally ebbed, what remained were the stories: raw, tragic, and human. The scale shrank suddenly from the expansive to the intimate. I found myself in a room with a woman and senior police officers. I could smell the metallic scent of weapons in the air, the sweat of exhaustion, and the heavy silence: that unspoken weight of everything we had just witnessed, everything too large for words.

The interview began. I felt the gravity of the operation pressing down on me, the weight of all that had been uncovered. The conversation flowed through me: details, statistics, statements. My notebook filled with shorthand facts, my voice steady, precise.

And then it shifted. Out came the human experiences, the impossible choices, the tangled lives unravelling before us. Words buzzing in my ears, echoing inside my skull.

During the entire interview, I had avoided eye contact whenever the emotions threatened to overwhelm me. It was my silent tactic, to coach myself in the shadows, telling my body to calm down, to breathe, and to keep going. I wanted to get the job done. Done well. Done professionally.

And then it happened. A flickering disturbance in an officer's eye. Not indifference, not coldness, but deep emotions straining against the surface. In that split second, I recognised it: the reflection of a fellow human being, also acting as a professional, also trying to contain what could not be contained. That look blasted through the last line of defence I had left. My professional armour cracked wide open. My emotions burst out of me. Hot tears streamed down my face. I tried to keep speaking, to keep the sentences flowing, but my voice faltered. My body shook. I was crying so much I could no longer string my sentences together. My chest heaved with convulsive sobs, gasping for air, as if my body itself had been hijacked. I curled into my chair, almost in a fetal position. My shorthand notes blurred beneath the falling tears. My voice collapsed.

And then something extraordinary happened. The officers began to cry. One, then two, and soon all of them: men and women alike. Some cried silently, stood up and walked to the side. Others, like me, gasped for air between sobs. The woman we were there to question wept openly.

We had to call for a break: an unplanned pause in the middle of that heavy room. We stepped outside, gulping fresh air, trying to recollect ourselves. Slowly, layer by layer, we began to pull the armour of professionalism back on, preparing to return to the task.

In that room, professionalism had shattered, composure had dissolved. And yet when the break ended, we did what professionals do: we carried on.

But something had shifted. In breaking down, I had glimpsed something I hadn't expected: the cost of perfect invisibility. The price of being emotionally transparent wasn't just professional, it was personal. Years of absorbing without processing, of witnessing without feeling, of being present without being seen, had hollowed me out from the inside.

I would never forget the truth that broke through in that moment—we were human, all of us. And no amount of professional training could, and frankly, should change us.

That day marked the beginning of a question I wasn't yet ready to ask: What happens to the parts of yourself you're trained to silence? Where do they go? And after years of practised invisibility, who are you when no one is watching?

Key Moments

- Interpreting put me at the centre of events, but silenced my voice.

- Training demanded I absorb everything, express nothing.

- The better I performed, the less of me remained.

- One glance cracked my armour, and the tears came.

- Invisibility's cost: erase yourself too long, and you lose who you are.

My favourite photo of me and grandma.

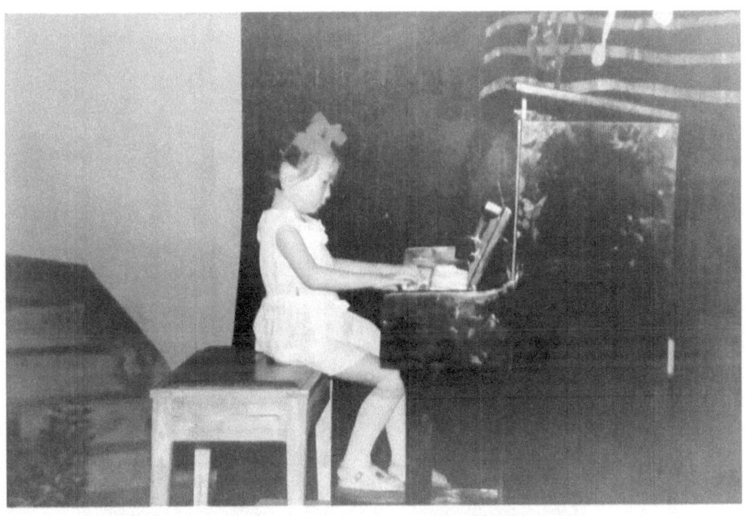

One of my first public performances,
when my feet could not touch the floor,
and had to rest on a foot stool.

This used to be my hiding space (on the stage).

Recording time (and learning
perfection did not exist).

Receiving my PhD: a moment to
behold (for me and my family).

Chapter 5

The Quiet Collapse

And then, one day, the show ended.

When COVID arrived, everything stopped. There were no stages, no audiences, no international summits. No applause, no compliments, no satin dresses or rehearsed lines or tightly timed cues.

The world had shrunk to the walls of our home. Outside, an invisible virus hung in the air: one that could kill, that spread through breath, touch, proximity. Inside, the silence was punctured only by the endless doomsday reports crackling from the radio. Twenty-four-hour news cycles that I couldn't turn off but had no time to process. I kept hearing about musicians changing careers, industry leaders moving countries, music institutions letting whole staffs go.

No visitors allowed, no grandparents to hold the baby, no casual encounters that once made life feel connected and alive. Just the relentless updates of death tolls, lockdown extensions, economic collapse. Would this last months? Years? Would our industries survive? Would we?

In the midst of navigating this new reality—juggling the isolation, the fear, the constant need to shield my children from the chaos: we were also living in our dream house while it was still under construction. With a newborn and a toddler demanding everything I had, my world had contracted to the most essential elements. There was only this: incomplete construction tasks scattered throughout rooms, unpacked boxes stacked in corners, nappies everywhere. A body stretched by motherhood, slowed by fatigue. And a mind no longer capable of delivering on command or of imagining what came next.

I was no longer the high-achieving, polished professional. I was a scruffy, milk-stained, sleep-deprived woman trying to keep a new life nourished and another small human entertained, while the world unravelled outside and the future seemed more confusing than ever.

A dream house, yes. But also a burden. Financially. Emotionally. And logistically.

My husband was equally overwhelmed, building his business while managing house construction. We were both drowning in our separate responsibilities, but there was no time to even acknowledge it.

What had once been a symbol of vision and arrival: our dream house, began to feel like another form of performance, another script I had inherited and absorbed. It was only through the compliments and over-the-top praise about our house that I realised we had built for the approval of others rather than our own needs. We were pouring our energy and savings into something we had once longed for. And yet, as we progressed, I began to wonder: Was this dream even mine? Or just another box to tick, another expectation to fulfill?

Because while the show had stopped, the audience had vanished too. And the one observer I disappointed most, was myself.

I despised the version of me that had emerged. Not because she was raw or tired or imperfect, but because she was so ineffective. So unproductive. So far from the polished woman I had always been proud to present.

I saw her in the mirror each morning: the exhausted woman with swollen eyes, wearing yesterday's T-shirt, trying to find the stamina to finish a sentence, let alone hold a conversation. She was the one my tired husband spoke to each evening. The one my aging parents now worried about instead of took pride in. The one who no longer inspired, no longer impressed, and not even herself.

No applause. No measurable results. No rhythm. No routine. Just the blurry, monotonous stillness of survival.

In the midst of all this chaos, I poured my work energy into teaching. Something I had always treasured. Many of my prolific performer friends and colleagues often questioned: "How do you do it? Where do you get the patience from?" I had dreamt of being a teacher since I was three years old, perhaps even before I asked my parents for a "real piano".

I loved not only the art of understanding people's challenges and problems, but also finding the most effective, concise, and relatable ways to make ideas understood, strategies applied, and motivation restored. Beyond that, I loved the emotional exchange: helping students understand their personal learning habits, comprehension blocks, and deeply-rooted fears. During COVID lockdowns, house relocations, new motherhood, and maternity leaves, teaching became my constant. It kept me sane, kept me purposeful, creative, motivated. It even gave me a routine and paid the bills!

But even in teaching—the one area that still felt authentic, I began to question myself.

When the Music Stopped

And then came the part that frightened me the most.

I could no longer listen to piano music, not even on the radio. I would hear a few notes and turn it off, as if the sound itself could pierce me open. Classical music, once my refuge, now felt unbearable. I couldn't bear to hear of friends or acquaintances breaking records, releasing albums, leading world-class projects in some other corners of the world.

I couldn't touch the piano. I couldn't play. My fingers, once so fluent, felt like strangers.

There was a moment (quiet, uneventful on the outside), when I sat alone in our unfinished home, I realised I no longer recognised my own life.

I was at the bottom. Nothing made sense. I couldn't see my next step, let alone the road ahead. My mind was full, cluttered with noise, responsibility, resentment, regret. I felt heavy, flat, and raw. The kind of raw that doesn't inspire growth, only retreat.

When My Body Spoke

And my body... my body was aching.

Every morning I would wake up sore, unrested. My bones felt like they'd aged decades overnight. I'd go to bed early, desperate for a long, healing sleep, each morning I woke up with the same dull heaviness in my head, the same resistance in my limbs. I'd lie there, staring at the ceiling, willing myself to get up, to start again. But my body refused.

It ached not from a workout or a virus or poor posture. It ached from witnessing everything.

At the time, I didn't know. I blamed it on child-bearing, heavy lifting, moving house. Maybe I was pre-menopausal. Maybe I needed more magnesium, more sleep, more exercise, more something.

But in hindsight, I know the truth. My body was keeping the score.

It was holding the tension, the grief, the pressure, the self-betrayal. Every muscle had something to say, and I wasn't listening. My body had become the loudest voice in my life, and I kept shushing it, ignoring the signals, pushing through.

The Voice I Couldn't Hear

For years, I had been fluent in every language except the one my own body spoke.

I could interpret complex diplomatic conversations, decode musical scores, read rooms full of strangers, but I couldn't read my own signals. I had been trained, like most high-achievers, to override. To push through. To treat my body like a servant that should work overtime without complaint.

But bodies don't negotiate. They don't send written warnings. They just get louder and louder until you have no choice but to hear.

Lying there each morning, staring at the ceiling, I began to understand something that terrified me: my body had been trying to communicate with me for years. The tight shoulders. The shallow breathing. The exhaustion that came not after exertion, but after forcing myself to do things that felt wrong.

I had been so busy performing, so focused on external applause, and so drawn to producing, projecting and fitting in. And I had become completely deaf to my own inner orchestra.

Burning Too Bright

In my motherhood, I found myself caught between worlds. A part of me loved meeting fellow parents, especially other new mothers. There was comfort in the shared experience, weekly meetups, spontaneous playdates, endless messages in group chats. We laughed, we vented, we compared baby milestones and swapped half-eaten snacks in playgrounds. In the middle of that cheerful noise, there were moments that stole my breath, my child's warm palm finding mine on the walk home, milk breath on my collarbone at three in the morning, the lemon scent of a small head beneath my kiss. That quiet devotion gently blew me away.

But another part of me stood slightly outside it all, observant and quiet. A large, vital part, one that remained untapped in these conversations. While some mothers shared how becoming a mother was the ultimate fulfillment, a major life upgrade, a dream come true, the best thing that ever happened to them, I often found myself nodding along, genuinely moved by their joy, while my truth stayed unspoken.

I loved my children fiercely. Motherhood was wondrous, transformative, and irreplaceable. But it wasn't *the* defining achievement of my life. It was a profound chapter, not the entire story. A beautiful transformation, not an identity takeover.

I couldn't find the words to express this distinction without sounding ungrateful or diminishing what motherhood meant to others (and to me). I just firmly and quietly believed that loving your children deeply and needing more than motherhood to feel whole, could coexist.

Then came the moments that confirmed my isolation.

During one of the lockdowns, someone asked: "How are you and your kids?" Before I could answer, she said: "Well, you timed it well. If there is any good time to have kids, it is now during COVID, isn't it?"

The casual dismissal was breathtaking.

Then another day, in a group setting, the conversation turned to life beyond maternity leave. Some spoke of negotiating part-time roles. Others talked about the need to slow down or shift priorities. I found myself engaged, enjoying the openness, feeling like I could contribute authentically. When it was my turn, I shared that I was excited to return to more teaching, and was also exploring the right time to resume performing and touring.

One mother turned to me, looked into my eyes, and said flatly: "Well, listen to you! You're so funny!"

Silence. The group went still. Some froze, some looked away. Nobody spoke up.

It stung.

I didn't know what she meant exactly, but the tone said everything. Too ambitious. Too much. Too "other". Her words dismissed my reality and in doing so, dismissed me. I had learnt something painful about listening: Sometimes the deepest loneliness comes not from being unheard, but from having no one to hear you fully.

The dismissal hit harder because it came from someone I had hoped would understand. In a moment when I was already questioning every part of my identity, her mockery confirmed my deepest fear: that there was no place for the fullness of who I was. That I had to choose. Be a mother OR be a devoted professional, fit in OR stand out, but never both.

It made me feel incompetent for any role: not mother enough, not professional enough, not woman enough.

What I was learning, painfully, was that I needed someone to really listen to me. Not to fix me, not to judge me, not to offer solutions. Just to hear me. To see the full picture of who I was trying to be.

But in my isolation, with toddler tantrums and feeding schedules consuming every moment, that kind of listening felt impossible to find. I was drowning in the very life I had thought I wanted, surrounded by beautiful things that felt empty, holding roles that no longer fit.

I was lost. And alone. But still smiling.

Too Dim to Shine

The dismissals didn't only come from my parenting circles. They also came from elsewhere, casual and cutting.

One afternoon when restrictions had briefly lifted, I crossed paths with a neighbour during a walk in the park. Children ran across the grass while parents stood in careful clusters, desperate for connection after weeks of isolation. I was pushing the pram when she approached: someone's mum from the neighbourhood. She had a well-meaning brightness that mothers often bring to casual encounters.

"Hi Zen! What are you up to these days?"

I smiled. "I've been teaching."

"Oh! Like... music lessons?"

I nodded.

She paused, and I could see her reconciling this with what she remembered of my earlier career. "You could have done such great things with all your talent," she said, then asked: "Are you happy just teaching?"

The word hung in the air. *Just.*

I knew she didn't mean it cruelly. She was someone who wore her heart on her sleeve, and in her mind, she was probably expressing concern, wondering if I'd had to let go of dreams she remembered me having. Her question reflected her image of who I'd been, what she'd expected I would become.

"Oh no, I really do love it," I said, laughing a little.

But even as the words left my mouth, something inside me was collapsing. She'd already moved on to lighter conversation, but I stood there nodding along, that single word tightening in my chest.

Just... a teacher.

As I walked home pushing the pram, a deeper sadness settled in. Not anger at her, she couldn't have known how fragile I already felt, but a grief I couldn't yet name.

It would take me months to understand what her question had actually touched. In hindsight, I realised the pain wasn't that I had started doubting teaching when others showed disapproval. Teaching was vital, meaningful work that I genuinely loved. The pain was that her words exposed something I'd been trying not to see: my other talents—performing, building cultural bridges, the parts of me that had once felt so alive, were lying dormant. Unfulfilled. Unused. And I had been aware of that all along.

Her question didn't make me question teaching. It made me confront how much of myself I had set aside.

But I wasn't ready to face that yet. So instead, I absorbed her doubt as a referendum on teaching itself. I told myself the work I was doing wasn't enough, rather than admitting I needed more expressions of who I was.

The irony cut deep. In my darkest moments, teaching had been my lifeline. When I could barely recognise myself, the connection with my students remained authentic. Watching fear transform into confidence, witnessing someone discover their capability, that magic never lied. Teaching wasn't the problem. It was never the problem.

But her question, well-intentioned as it may have been, seeded a confusion I couldn't yet untangle. I began explaining my choices defensively: "I'm teaching, and I'm too busy to return to other things". I questioned whether teaching diminished my credibility as a performer, whether being an expert somehow meant I shouldn't also teach that craft.

The woman who had once commanded concert halls was now apologising for work she loved. Not because teaching was insufficient, but because she hadn't yet given herself permission to be more than one thing.

The Final Reckoning

Those confronting and heart-wrenching encounters, had been adding up. Layer by layer, they had built something I didn't recognise: doubt where there had once been certainty, shame where there had once been pride.

I found myself caught in an impossible place. Too ambitious for the mothers who wanted me to fit in. Too settled for those who remembered my former glory. Too bright for some, too dimmed for others. And now, finally, too withered to glow at all.

The woman who had once lit up concert halls was now struggling to light up her own life. I moved through my days like a sleepwalker, going through the motions but no longer fully inhabiting them. The vibrancy that had once been my signature was fading, dimmed by the constant message that nothing I chose was ever quite right.

And in that dimness, something profound began to happen. I realised I had stopped listening, to things that truly mattered.

I couldn't bear piano music anymore. I wasn't hearing my body's alarms. My own voice had gone silent beneath everyone else's expectations. And no one was truly listening to me either.

For someone who had devoted decades to the art of listening—to music, to language, to the spaces between words, I had become profoundly deaf to what mattered most.

In the space where my old certainties had lived, where external validation had once roared its approval or disapproval, I finally became quiet enough to hear my own voice. And this time, I was ready to listen, deeply.

The Dots You Can Only See Looking Back

I wish I could tell you that in that moment, sitting in the car with tears streaming down my face, I had a plan. That I could see the path ahead clearly, know exactly what needed to change, or understand the journey I was about to begin.

But that's not how transformation works.

Steve Jobs once said that you can't connect the dots looking forward, you can only connect them looking backward. And he was right. When you're in the collapse, when everything you've built is crumbling, when the old certainties no longer hold, there are no dots to see. There's only the fog, the grief, and the terrifying question: *Now what?*

I had always been a learner. Introspective, curious, hungry for understanding. I'd read voraciously, sought mentors, pursued knowledge with the same intensity I brought to everything else. But here's what was different now: I surrendered to imperfection.

For the first time in my life, I wasn't learning to become flawless. I was learning to be ME. I stopped trying to fix what was broken and started listening to what was true and aligned. I kept pursuing excellence (that drive never left me), but now it was tethered to an authentic self, not a performed one.

I invested in myself differently. Not just professionally, as I had always done, but personally. For me. For the human being who lived inside this highly-wired body, beneath the credentials and the accomplishments and the carefully curated persona. I sought mentors who could see my humanity beyond my potential. I gave myself permission for imperfect progress. I read books that challenged me to feel, not just think. I allowed myself to be a student of my own life.

And slowly, through that surrender, through learning to pursue excellence with imperfection rather than despite it, something began to emerge.

What I didn't know then was that this collapse of listening would become the foundation for everything that followed. Years later, I would realise that this moment contained two essential lessons: one about listening outward, one about listening inward.

The first would become my **T.U.N.E. framework**: the art of Deep Listening that transforms how we connect with others, how we lead, how we show up in our relationships. T.U.N.E.—Tune In, Unlock Curiosity, Nurture Connection, Elevate Communication. It teaches the practice of listening that goes beyond hearing words to truly understanding what's being communicated. Because I learned the hard way that you can't truly hear another person when you're drowning in your own noise.

The second would become my **S.T.A.G.E. framework**: the inner journey from perfection to freedom, from performance to authentic presence. The path through Stillness, Truth, Alignment, Growth, and Expression—each stage a lesson I would learn by walking through this collapse and choosing to rebuild differently.

Both frameworks emerged from the same crisis, distilled from the same personal journey, and both are essential. But I came to understand something crucial: I couldn't teach others to listen deeply until I learned to listen to myself. T.U.N.E. became possible only after I walked through S.T.A.G.E.

This book is the story of that inner journey—the one that had to come first. The journey through collapse and stillness, through hard truths and painful alignment, through growth that felt more like unlearning, and finally to expression that was real, not performed.

It would be months, maybe years, before I could look back and see the pattern. Before I could name what had carried me from that car park to the life I live now. Before I understood that what felt like chaos was actually, a part of the life symphony.

S.T.A.G.E. Not only because I love this acronym, but also because the word itself held meaning for me. As a performer, the stage had always been where I proved my worth, where I became visible, where I was judged and celebrated. But this stage would be different. This would be the stage of my becoming—not a platform for performance, but a structure for transformation.

S — STILLNESS: The forced pause that became sacred space

T — TRUTH: The reckoning with what was real, not perfect

A — ALIGNMENT: The integration of values with action

G — GROWTH: The expansion beyond old identities

E — EXPRESSION: The courage to show up as myself

I didn't move through these stages cleanly or sequentially. I circled back through them. I resisted them. Some lasted weeks, others stretched across seasons. But each one changed me. Each one taught me something I couldn't have learned any other way.

This is the story of how I moved through each stage. How they dismantled me and rebuilt me.

How they asked everything of me and gave me back myself.

The dots only connect looking backward. But once you see them, once you understand the pattern, you realise: you weren't falling apart.

You were breaking open.

Key Moments

- COVID stopped the show. My body disobeyed. My world shrank to silence.

- Dismissals accumulated from all sides: too much, too little, never quite right.

- The deepest loneliness: having no one to hear you fully.

- "Are you happy just teaching?" hurt because my other talents were dormant, not because teaching was lesser.

- I had stopped listening—to everything that mattered. Expert listener, profoundly deaf to myself.

- Two frameworks born from collapse: **T.U.N.E.** (listening outward), **S.T.A.G.E.** (listening inward).

- You can't listen deeply to others until you learn to listen to yourself.

- I wasn't falling apart. I was breaking open.

Chapter 6

Stillness

Every musician knows that in music, rests are as important as the notes.

A rest isn't an empty space, it's intentional silence. It gives the sound time to resonate, the listener time to absorb, the performer time to breathe. Without rests, music becomes noise. The notes blur together, meaning dissolves, and eventually, even the most beautiful melody becomes unbearable.

I had been playing the 'symphony of my life' without rests for decades.

When the music finally stopped, not by choice, but by collapse, I didn't recognise the silence as salvation. I experienced it as punishment. Emptiness. Failure. The absence of everything I'd built my identity upon.

But stillness, I would learn, wasn't the absence of anything. It was the presence of meaning, space, and abundance—and it allowed me to access something I'd lost: myself.

Yet discovering that I needed stillness didn't tell me what to do with it. I had space, but no roadmap. Silence, but no answers. Time, but no structure to hold it.

What followed was a journey I hadn't anticipated: one that moved through resistance, discovery, searching, and finally, revelation. This is the story of what happened when I finally stopped running.

When Stillness Arrives Uninvited

Most of us say we value stillness. We speak about pausing, about taking a breath. We know it matters in theory.

But knowing and living are not the same.

I was busy chasing excellence. Having it all. Showing up for everyone. I built a life on competence and control. Until one day, it collapsed.

From the outside, no one saw it. There were no headlines, no scandal. But inside, my entire world crumbled.

The crash felt like being slammed into an uninvited rest in the score, one I hadn't rehearsed for, but deeply needed. What shocked me most wasn't the external chaos. It was my body. My limbs heavy. My muscles aching. My breath shallow. It was as if my body had finally caught up with the emotional cost of years of performance without pause.

Stillness didn't arrive as a soft reprieve. It arrived as a reckoning.

The irony was sharp. For years I had taught my students that silence is the soul, the alma, of every phrase. That rests give music meaning. That without pause, there can be no shape, no depth, no truth.

And yet, I hadn't lived by my own teaching.

I romanticised stillness artistically, but refused to inhabit it personally. I taught others to honour the pause while I rushed past my own. I told students that silence separates the competent from the extraordinary, but I wouldn't let myself go there.

But when life forces the pause, when your body makes the choice your mind refused, you have two options: continue to resist, or finally surrender.

Slowly, reluctantly, I stopped fighting it.

Meeting Myself Again

When everything fell away, I dropped the obligation to impress. For the first time in years, I was alone with myself. It felt raw, like meeting an old friend after a long estrangement.

Questions rose like unresolved chords: What happened? Where are you now? What's left of you? How do you move forward?

As the days slowed, small treasures began to surface. The afternoon light spilling across the living room floor, dancing through the construction dust that still lingered in corners of our half-finished dream house. The magnolia blooming at the fence, somehow thriving despite the chaos of renovation around it. My children's innocent, piercing questions that cut straight to truth: "Why do adults always say, hurry up?" and "Why do you work?".

Questions I couldn't answer. Not because I didn't know the practical reasons, but because I suddenly couldn't remember the deeper why. When had my work become something I did to them instead of for them? When had urgency replaced presence as my default setting?

I heard them differently, because I finally left space for them to be heard.

I looked at my home not as a backdrop to busyness but as a chosen place, built with love, even if still incomplete. Boxes still waited to be unpacked, walls remained unfinished, but suddenly I could see the beauty in the becoming. And then it struck me: had I already held what I'd been chasing, but been too hurried to notice?

One morning, still in my pyjamas, I opened my wardrobe without the will to dress. Rows of carefully curated pieces greeted me: jackets from Tokyo, scarves from Florence, a clutch from Marrakech. Souvenirs from another life, another tempo.

Nearby, awards and certificates stared back quietly, asking: What now? Were they proof of a joyous life, or evidence of success?

I didn't know. But I finally had the space to ask.

The questions accumulated. They filled the quiet. And while I could sit with them in my own company, I also felt the pull to seek guidance beyond myself. Not answers, exactly—but wisdom. A framework. Something to help me make sense of what I was discovering.

The Search for Solid Ground

I didn't know what I was searching for, only that I had to look. I joined dance groups, book clubs, meditation circles. I slipped into Catholic masses, Buddhist talks, somatic workshops, hoping rituals and structures might whisper wisdom. Nothing quite landed.

I wasn't seeking religion, not really. I was searching for something to hold me. Something to remind me of what mattered. Something to tether me to the present in a way achievement never could.

Everything felt either too rigid or too distant, too loud or too abstract, none of it was quite for ME and for NOW.

One afternoon, desperate for fresh air and some clarity when nothing was clear and I didn't know where to look or how to gather my thoughts, I walked to the Yarra River.

The Tree

The path was familiar, but I felt like a stranger in my own city.

And then I saw it: a tree split cleanly in half, perhaps by lightning or storm. One side was completely dead: bark peeling, branches brittle and lifeless. But the other side was magnificently alive, shooting toward the sky with vibrant green leaves, as if freed by the death of its other half to reach its full potential.

I stood there staring at this tree for a long time. I didn't fully understand what it was showing me yet. But something in me recognised it: a truth I wasn't ready to name, but needed to see.

What Stillness Taught Me

That tree stayed with me. In the days that followed, I began to understand what it was showing me: not just about loss and growth, but about the stillness I'd been resisting.

The tree didn't choose which side lived and which side died. It simply stopped fighting what had already happened and poured its energy into what remained. In the same way, stillness asked me to stop resisting what was beneath the rubble, and start noticing what remained.

And what I found surprised me.

First came awareness. Not the sharp, strategic awareness I'd honed as a performer, always scanning for cues and reactions. This was softer, inward-facing. I became aware of my breathing—how shallow it had become. The tension I held in my shoulders, even in sleep. How often I interrupted my own thoughts with *should* and *must* and *have to*. For the first time in years, I was listening to my body's signals instead of overriding them.

Then, unexpectedly, came curiosity. For years, I had been certain about everything: my path, my purpose, my next achievement, and what defines excellence. But in stillness, I discovered the grace of not knowing. Who was I when no one was watching? What did I actually enjoy when I wasn't performing enjoyment? What mattered to me versus what I thought should matter? These weren't questions to solve, but invitations to explore.

With curiosity came something I had rarely allowed myself: self-empathy. I had always been my harshest critic, my most demanding teacher. But lying there, exhausted and empty, I finally saw myself as I would see a dear friend in pain. That woman who had pushed so hard, performed so perfectly, carried so much. She wasn't weak for collapsing. She was human. And she deserved compassion, especially from herself.

And then came the most confronting recognition: my ego had been running the show. Not in the obvious, boastful way, but in the constant need to be useful, impressive, beyond reproach. My ego had convinced me that my worth was my performance. That love was earned through excellence. That rest was laziness and vulnerability was danger. In the stillness, I could finally see it clearly: this exhausting inner taskmaster that had been driving me for decades.

The stillness also revealed something deeper: the weight I'd been carrying wasn't only mine. I was shouldering the burden of generations. My grandmother's silencing. My mother's stolen opportunities. The family trauma that taught us to be excellent but invisible, brilliant but never threatening. I had absorbed their unfulfilled dreams alongside my own ambitions, their fears woven into my drive. No wonder I was exhausted. I was living multiple lives at once, carrying not just my own expectations but theirs too.

Stillness didn't give me answers. But it gave me something more valuable: the capacity to see clearly. To distinguish between what was mine to carry and what I'd inherited.

Understanding what I'd been carrying was one thing. Setting it down was another. And that practice began with the simplest, most physical act: opening my hands.

Opening My Hands

Stillness doesn't just open your eyes. It opens your hands.

I always admired Marie Kondo's approach to decluttering by asking this simple question: Does this spark joy? For years, I'd applied it to clothing and clutter. But now, in this season of forced stillness, the question became larger and more terrifying. It wasn't just about objects anymore. It was about everything I was carrying.

In the quiet, I realised how much I was carrying: objects, expectations, old ambitions, and unspoken grief. So much weight I had normalised, like background noise in a score. Even the cruel words from that stranger in the car park, calling me "stupid"—I had been carrying those too, letting them echo in the spaces where self-doubt already lived.

I began to understand that letting go wasn't just about decluttering objects. It was about releasing what no longer served the woman I was becoming.

So I began.

Not as a lifestyle trend, but as survival. First, the small things: notebooks, scarves, dishes I never used. Then harder ones: unopened gifts, books bought to impress, shoes that hurt but looked "glamorous".

Each object was a note I had once chosen. Some harmonised with who I was now. Others clashed with who I was becoming. All made me ask: *Does this still spark joy? Does this still belong in the music of my life?*

I released designer pieces that belonged to another version of myself. Old performance programmes I could barely remember. Documents I'd hoarded out of fear I might need to prove something someday. I said no to commitments I once accepted out of guilt, habit, or the fear of being forgotten.

I stopped measuring worth in checklists. Instead, I asked a quieter question: *Does this bring me closer to who I really am now?*

It wasn't glamorous. It wasn't linear. Some days I clung desperately to what I was releasing. Other days I wanted to burn everything down and start from nothing. But slowly, a rhythm returned—not erasure, but composition. A slower, more deliberate score.

Letting go brought discomfort and grief, but also relief and hope: the release of a long, withheld rest.

The Music Between the Notes

In music, resonance depends on space. A violin cannot truly sing if its strings are too tight, a music composition does not communicate true emotions when it is packed with notes with little rest, a fast passage is soulless if it is merely a show of virtuosity, not serving a bigger emotional picture.

The same is true of a life.

Stillness taught me that resonance requires room. Not every note belongs. Not every phrase can be sustained. Not every beautiful sound must continue forever.

Travelling light didn't mean giving up ambition. It meant choosing carefully which notes to keep, which silences to honour, and which movements to carry forward into whatever came next.

Like that tree by the Yarra River, I was learning that sometimes the most radical act of growth is conscious release.

Because whether in music or in life, the rests are what make the melody whole.

Stillness gave me the space to listen again—not just to the world, but to myself. To hear my own voice beneath the noise of expectation. To feel my own rhythm beneath the tempo others had set for me.

And in that listening, I found what I'd been missing for years:

Space. Breath. Possibility.

Awareness without judgment. Curiosity without urgency. Compassion without conditions.

The capacity to choose not just what to add, but what to release. Not just what to become, but what to stop being. Not just how to fill the silence, but how to let it hold me.

The strings had been cut. The puppetry was over. For the first time in my life, I wasn't performing someone else's script or dancing to someone else's rhythm. I was ready to claim a stage of my own. Not as the polished performer, not as the perfect achiever, but as myself. Raw. Real. The master of my own life.

No more puppet strings. No more invisible hands directing my movements.

Just me, standing in my own truth, ready to write my own score.

In that stillness, something new could finally begin.

Key Moments

- Rests in music aren't empty—they're where meaning settles.

- I had been playing the symphony of my life without rests for decades.

- Stillness arrived not as salvation but as punishment, until I stopped resisting it.

- Meeting myself again felt like encountering an old friend after long estrangement.

- I searched for solid ground in dance groups, meditation circles, religious services. Nothing landed.

- Then I saw the split tree: one side dead, the other magnificently alive, freed by loss to reach its potential.

- Stillness taught me awareness, curiosity, self-empathy, and revealed my ego's grip and my ancestors' weight.

- Letting go wasn't just about objects. It was about releasing what no longer served who I was becoming.

- Like a violin's strings, life needs space to resonate. Not every note belongs.

- The rests are what make the melody whole.

My practices

- Every week, I release or re-negotiate one thing that no longer sparks joy.

- Each day I add a three-minute buffer between two tasks.

- When tension rises, I take two rounds of breathing: four in, six out, then choose.

Chapter 7

Truth

In the stillness, I had found space. I had learned to listen. I had opened my hands and let go of what no longer served me.

But stillness, for all its gifts, had also left me in an uncomfortable place: the space between who I had been and who I was becoming. Neither here nor there. No longer performing, but not yet certain what came next.

My grandmother used to say, "When an animal is pushed into a corner, it does one of two things: it folds in on itself and waits, or it leaps, claws out, and carves its way back into the world".

I did not know it then, but her words wrote themselves into me. Survival once felt certain. What I wanted now was truth. I began with the part of me that could not pretend.

The Truth About the Body

My body spoke first. It started with whispers, then with shouts. Sore bones at dawn. A clenched jaw through sleep. Breath that barely reached the ribs. I blamed mattresses, hormones, posture, and the pace of life. I treated my body like a machine that needed resets. Massages. Retreats. Classes. Helpful at times, but the signals didn't stop. The pain kept speaking.

And that's when I realised: the pain was not asking to be treated. It was asking to be heard.

For years, I had been the CEO of my body in name only. I measured output and ignored warning lights. I praised productivity and punished fatigue. I drove performance without checking capacity. My body wasn't broken. It was protesting. And what I'd called "pushing through" was actually a systematic muting of my own life force.

The truth was uncomfortable but undeniable: I had been an absent leader. I had overridden signals, dismissed complaints, and silenced objections. All in service of an agenda my body never agreed to.

So I made a decision. I would start listening. Not with quick fixes or temporary relief, but with genuine attention. Daily, sustainable care. I would treat my body not as a servant to override, but as a partner to respect.

The truth about my body changed everything. Because once I heard it, I couldn't unhear it.

The Truth About Time

Time had become my currency. I could stack schedules, cross continents, deliver on cue, then answer everyone by nightfall. My calendar was a mosaic of achievement blocks, each one proof of my productivity, my worth.

Then came the enforced pause.

And in that stillness, time became something different: not a resource to manage, but a mirror. When I looked at how I'd actually spent my days, weeks, years, the dissonance was impossible to ignore.

I had accomplished a great deal. But how much of it had been aligned with what actually mattered? How much had been driven by Should rather than Want? By fear of disappointing others rather than devotion to myself?

I was so skilled at filling time that I'd forgotten to live in it.

The truth was uncomfortable: I had treated time like something to conquer rather than something to inhabit. I measured my days by what I'd crossed off, not by who I'd been while doing it. Every hour had been accounted for, but few had been truly lived.

I couldn't possess time. I could only choose how to honour it.

So I began to ask different questions. Not *What did I get done today?* but *Who was I while doing it?* Not *How much did I accomplish?* but *How did that just nourish me?*

This was the truth about time: it would pass whether I rushed through it or moved with intention. The only choice I had was how I wanted to meet it.

The Truth About Self

When I slowed enough to see not only my days but my years, another truth surfaced—perhaps the most uncomfortable one yet.

Much of what I chased was not born from my deepest desires. It was built to meet a perceived expectation. A dream house. A respected profession. A global footprint. The useful, impressive life. None of it was false—I had wanted these things. But I had wanted them, at least in part, because I thought they proved something. To my family. To my world. To myself.

Conditioning had done its quiet work.

So I began asking different questions. What would I pursue if no one was watching? What would I build if admiration did not factor in? What would feel successful even in secret?

The answers weren't immediate. But the questions themselves revealed something: I had been performing a version of success rather than living one that felt true.

And then I saw the deeper pattern—the one I'd inherited.

I came to realise that I carried a family story that feared of being both too bright and too dim. Be brilliant, but discreetly. Shine, but don't be too bright. Rise, but don't risk safety. My grandmother had been publicly humiliated for her education. My mother had been denied hers entirely. They had learned, painfully, that visibility could be dangerous.

So they taught me to succeed, but to do it carefully. Excel, but don't draw attention. Lead, but don't call yourself a leader. Achieve, but never at the cost of safety, belonging, or approval.

I had absorbed both messages: be exceptional *and* invisible. No wonder I felt perpetually split—too much for some, too little for others, never quite right for anyone.

And then came the realisation that changed everything.

In order to heal as a family, to thrive as my authentic self, and to give my children something freer, I had to do something that felt both honouring and heartbreaking: I had to acknowledge my ancestors' hardships while releasing their suffering.

I could carry their love forward without carrying their fear. I could honour their sacrifices without repeating their self-silencing. I could respect what they endured while refusing to let trauma become my inheritance.

Their pain was real. Their caution was earned. But it didn't have to be mine. Not anymore.

For the first time in a long time, I was willing to put the performance down. Not the excellence—I would always value that. But the need to calibrate my brightness to others' comfort. The exhausting dance of being impressive without being threatening.

The truth about myself was this: I had been living for an audience that was no longer in the room. And I was ready to stop.

The Truth About Relationships

As I began to see myself more clearly, I also began to see my relationships differently.

I had always prided myself on connection: my warmth, my people sense, my ability to build bonds. But in the stillness, I started asking harder questions.

Who actually saw me, versus who saw my usefulness? Which relationships were nourished by mutual care, and which ran on momentum alone? When I spent time with certain people, did I leave feeling more present or more performed?

The answers were revealing. Some relationships had been built on an older version of me: the high-achieving, always-available woman, who solved problems and opened doors. And here was the pattern I couldn't ignore: these were somewhat the same people who didn't know what to do with me when I'd silently collapsed, when the glamour was nowhere to be seen. And now, as I was rebuilding:

quieter, more boundaried, more intentional—they still didn't know what to do with me.

The truth was stark: these relationships had only ever had room for one version of me. The impressive one. The useful one. The one who looked good from the outside.

They couldn't hold my collapse. And they couldn't hold my quiet becoming either.

I could release them with gratitude for what they'd been, without resentment for what they couldn't become. Because the limitation wasn't personal—it was structural. These connections had been built on performance, not presence. And I was no longer performing.

Other relationships deepened when I brought more truth. When I stopped performing competence and started sharing struggle. When I set boundaries instead of silently over-extending. These were the connections worth protecting.

I also had to face a harder truth: some relationships had taught me patterns I needed to unlearn. I had absorbed values, habits, and ways of being that weren't mine—simply through proximity. I had drifted from myself without realising it, shaped by circles that celebrated what I could do rather than who I was.

Sorting relationships wasn't about keeping a scorecard. It was about honouring what was real and releasing what had run its course. It was about choosing presence over performance, even in connection.

And that choice would be tested most deeply in the relationship that mattered most.

My marriage.

The Truth About Marriage

One of the relationships I couldn't ignore in this reckoning—perhaps the most important one—was my marriage.

I married a man who was my best friend. We laughed in sync, dreamed in tandem, solved problems like teammates in a championship game. We shared a love for good food, complex ideas, culture, travel, ambition. We could read each other's moods with a glance, decode a full sentence from the smallest twitch of the lips.

We were explorers. Creators. Planners. We didn't just fall in love—we partnered for the climb.

It felt like we were two strong mountaineers, roped together, conquering the most almighty mountain in the world. One vision. Double the effort. Double the resources. Double the capacity.

We trusted each other with the ascent. We believed we could have it all—if we worked hard enough and stayed the course.

And we did work hard. We did dream big.

But somewhere along the way, something shifted.

And it wasn't just a slow shift. It was sharper than that. Less like a change in rhythm and more like waking up and realising we weren't on the same ledge anymore. We hadn't fallen, but we weren't where we used to be.

We had been so focused on the climb, for the family, for the dream, for the vision, that we forgot to check in on the climbers.

We forgot to tend to the physical and emotional wear and tear. We stopped doing the inner work, of growing, unravelling, evolving together, not just side by side. And our milestones—awards, figures, projects, became stand-ins for intimacy. Proof of progress, but not necessarily connection.

In hindsight, I see it clearly.

We were evolving. But were we evolving *with* each other, or just *near* each other?

Stillness allowed truth-telling. I asked the same questions of our marriage that I was asking of my life. Does this still belong to us? What needs to change?

We halted and told the truth. We named what was real. No performance. No quick fixes. We asked: Who are we now? What still fits? What is mine to carry? What can we set down together?

But here's what I discovered through the uncertainty, the conflict, and the hurt: I still had my best friend on my team.

We learned that long-term relationships aren't accidents. They're intentional, loving decisions made over and over again. And we were lucky. Despite all, genuinely lucky. Because we were willing to do the work.

The truth about our marriage was this: it needed to be rebuilt, not rescued. And we were both ready to build.

The Truth About Motherhood

For years I believed motherhood was not for me. I did not feel the pull and refused to enter it half-heartedly. Then life shifted. I committed to a life with a man who wanted a family, and I chose it with him.

Pregnancy and those early years changed me. Formative. Humbling. Spiritual. Motherhood did not erase me. It revealed a love I did not know my body could hold.

I wanted to give my children the best of me and, like many women of high standards, I brought perfectionism to parenting. I knew intellectually children do not need perfect mothers, yet knowing is not the same as living with grace.

Even in sleepless months, soul-swallowing months, I never let go of my own dreams. Deep down, I still held onto who I was becoming in the world. What I longed to pursue. What I was here to contribute. That quiet fire didn't go out, it just flicked behind closed doors.

But the needs of my children were primal. Urgent. Cellular. I was their everything. I was theirs now.

And so I was squeezed, unrelentingly at times, into an impossible space. Bounced back and forth between two truths that wouldn't make room for each other.

On one side: duty, love, responsibility, guilt. On the other: ambition, pursuit, self-criticism, longing. And in the middle: me. Split. Stretched. Inadequate in both directions.

It felt like I was constantly falling short—under-resourced, under-talented, unqualified to fully inhabit either role: the primal mother, or the professional, high-achieving woman.

No one warned me how loud the guilt would be or how invisible the longing. Or how hard it would be to feel whole when every part of me belonged to someone else.

But then came the truth that changed everything.

The truth was this: my love and drive for each—for my children and for my own becoming, is wholesome and powerful. I would never be truly happy if I "sacrificed" one for the other. That sacrifice would erode both.

My children don't need a diminished mother. They need one who is fully alive. And my dreams don't require me to abandon love, they flourish when rooted in it.

What I came to understand was that each benefits from the wellness of the other. When I am present with my children, truly present, I am a better version of myself. And when I pursue my own growth and calling, I bring a fuller, more grounded presence back to them.

The 'either/or' I'd been living in was a lie. The truth was both/and.

I could love my children fiercely and still need more to feel whole. I could be devoted and also have dreams beyond motherhood. These weren't contradictions. They were the fullness of being human.

Slowly, I am learning how to honour both. Not perfectly. But honestly.

———

Every strand of truth, about body, time, self, relationships, marriage, and motherhood, brought me to the bare floor of my life. No roles to perform. No illusion to prop up. Just me, as I was.

In the end, every truth I uncovered brought me to the same place: a place of freedom, power and wholeness. Not the seamless perfection I had once pursued, but the integrated honesty of a woman who had finally stopped running from herself. The collapse hadn't just cleared the stage—it had revealed that I was both the stage and the performer, the music and the silence between the notes.

From here on, anything worth building would be built from truth.

What followed was not reinvention. It was remembering, of who I had been underneath the applause, of what I needed beneath the roles, and of the kind of strength that does not need to impress, only to feel right.

And from this place of truth, I was finally ready to do something I'd never done before: align my life with what I'd discovered.

Knowing the truth was one thing. Living it was another.

Key Moments

- **Body:** When something tightens, I treat it as information. One small change serves me today, whether sleep, load or pace.

- **Time:** A breath before each yes shows me if it fits this season. Small pauses shape the whole day.

- **Self:** I choose the path I would be proud of even if no one knew. It feels better than performing.

- **Relationships:** I notice how I feel after time together. Where I feel more myself, I stay. Where I perform, I step back.

- **Marriage:** For us, a healthy marriage means two people growing, healing and staying curious about each other. We hold a simple shared vision and talk early, plainly and often.

- **Repair:** Simple, specific words move us forward. I am sorry. I see what you carried. Here is what I can take today.

- **Motherhood:** My children notice presence more than perfection. I let them see me rest, repair and keep becoming.

- **Rhythm:** I put pauses in the calendar to keep aligned. Applause can wait.

Chapter 8

Alignment

There is an old story you have probably heard. A radiant bird, the phoenix, reaches the end of its life. Instead of fading quietly, it does something extraordinary. It builds a nest, lies down in it, and allows itself to burn. Completely. Intentionally. To ashes. When all is still, something stirs. From the ruins, a new phoenix rises. Not a replica of what it was, but something wiser, lighter, and more true. Born not in spite of the fire, but because of it.

It is a beautiful myth. Like many myths, it stays because it feels true. We all burn in our own way, and we all rise. What we rarely name is the small turning point between the two. Not the triumph, but the quiet return of energy. The moment when something inside begins to cohere again. When you sense, not because the world gives permission, but because something deep within says, *I am ready.*

That was me. After months of stillness, soul-searching, truth-telling, and the unravelling of everything I had been taught to be, something shifted. Nothing dramatic. No announcement. No sudden plan. A clarity formed, subtle and steady, like the first notes of a melody I had forgotten how to sing. My energy returned, not as adrenaline or performance, but as coherence. A gentle rhythm of alignment.

I began to see my life differently. Not as something to control or perfect, but as something to integrate. My instincts sharpened. My values spoke louder than my fears. I did not want to perform. I wanted to build. Not a stage, a life. It felt like lining up all the parts of myself: my voice, my experience, my gifts, my story, and letting them move in the same direction. This was alignment. The rise. Not of a brand or a new identity, but of something essential. Me.

Not the woman I tried to be. Not the polished achiever others expected. The woman who burned, surrendered, and survived, now standing barefoot in the ashes, ready to build from truth. There is a rare power in that. It does not shout. It does not seek validation. It moves with quiet certainty. Alignment did not feel like a battle won. It felt like coming home.

So I rose. Not to prove anything. Not to rebound into another role. I began again with clarity, with grace, and without apology.

Alignment of Time

One of the first things I examined was time. For years I spoke about priorities. I told others, and myself, what I valued most. Family. Arts. Health. Rest. Presence. Then I looked at my days. The dissonance was obvious. I was always busy, always responding, pouring myself into a thousand little things. The things I claimed mattered most were often waiting at the margins.

How we spend time is the most honest reflection of what we truly prioritise. Not what we aspire to value, but what we give ourselves to, day after day. Time does not lie. The more my schedule aligned with my truth, the more integrity I felt in my own skin.

During the late stages of my PhD, the project had become part of my identity. I said, day after day, with pride, *I am working on my PhD*. It carried prestige, effort and purpose. Then two years became three, four, and then the shadow of a fifth. Panic set in. I told myself I was failing. Perhaps the project had outgrown me. Perhaps I was not good enough to finish.

My boyfriend, who is now my husband, asked a simple question: "Do you think you actually prioritise your PhD?"

I bristled. "Of course. It is the most important pursuit in my life right now. I think about it all the time!"

He paused. "From what I see, it is not on your priority list at all. Not based on your time. You are always somewhere else, saying yes to everything and everyone, except the PhD. If it is not your priority, that is okay. Have you admitted that to yourself yet?"

He continued, gently. "You work on it if you have time. After you have given yourself to everything else, there is no time left. You say yes to everything, and what is left is not enough."

It hurt because he was right. My calendar told the truth. I was not giving the PhD the conditions it needed. It was living on scraps. The moment I faced that, everything changed. I reorganised my life. I protected time with intention. I said No to almost everything else. I shifted energy from talking to doing. In four months, I finished. Not a miracle of magic, but a practice of alignment.

Alignment of Habits

Next came my daily rhythm. I had long identified as a night owl. Late performances, long dinners, the best conversations after dark. It felt creative and a little luxurious. I told myself I was wired that way.

Then life asked for more clarity and steadiness. I began to question the rhythm. I shifted gently. Earlier nights. Earlier mornings. At first it felt awkward. Then I noticed the change. Mornings became clearer. My thinking sharpened. My energy evened out. Less swing between drama and depletion. I felt steady. Not glamorous, not exciting, simply aligned.

Alignment of Consumption

I came to understand that bodies are like gardens. If we want energy, focus, and clarity, we must tend the soil. Food, rest, and rhythm are acts of cultivation.

I looked closely at how I was eating. I was generally conscientious. Nourishing food. Not much intake of added sugar. Regular meals. Fine. But alignment does not stop at good enough. It asks what serves me now. In a season that demanded clarity and consistency, I experimented. I fine-tuned my food. I noticed how I felt after meals. I paid attention to what supported me and what quietly drained me. It was not a diet. It was listening.

Then there was alcohol. I have never been a big drinker. I enjoyed a toast, a beautiful glass, a cold beer on a hot day. During my season of depletion, I stopped completely. Not as a statement. My body simply said NO. I did not miss it. Later, when I tried a small sip, the feedback was immediate. Headache. Restless sleep. Waking in the night, wide awake and unsettled. Alcohol had never served me well. My awareness changed, and I finally accepted what I had ignored.

Consumption is not only physical. It is also what we allow into our minds. I turned off the background news. I stopped using talkback as company. I did not need constant updates or the emotional charge of headlines. I needed space. I asked, "What do I want to learn?" "What energy do I want around me?" Sometimes the answer was silence. Sometimes it was careful curation. I protected my mental environment with the same care I gave my body. What we consume shapes mood, focus, and spirit. The more I aligned what came in, the clearer I became.

Alignment in Relationships

As alignment grew inside me, I reviewed my relationships. Not only who I spent time with, but the ecosystem of obligations and rituals that once felt unquestionable.

Life is too short and too fragile to spend it curating other people's impressions. I had stretched myself thin, often in the name of generosity, sometimes in service of image. Helpful, impressive, available, accomplished. I kept moving to maintain a version of me.

In my season of collapse and stillness, the truth had crystallised. The people who showed up when I had nothing to offer, when I was not useful, fun, or impressive, were the ones to protect. The ones who circled only when the shine returned were not mine to carry.

Now, in alignment, I acted on that truth.

I let go of the belief that friendship requires constant tending to stay alive. I released the guilt of slower replies and fewer invitations accepted. I stopped confusing activity with intimacy. Being real, even respectfully blunt, became a form of kindness. Letting go, done with integrity, honours both sides. I stopped chasing connection that was not mutual. I stopped performing care when I needed solitude. Most importantly, I stopped dimming to fit people who preferred me smaller. I allowed myself to be seen as I am.

After everything, one truth stood firm. I am the CEO of my life. In a life built on alignment, there is no room for self-abandonment. Alignment is not a slogan. It is the daily act of letting time, habits, consumption, and relationships reflect what you truly value. It is the slow, steady rise after the fire. Not louder, but more grounded.

Alignment in Marriage

Understanding that our marriage needed rebuilding was one thing. Actually doing the work was another.

We faced what each of us brought from childhood. Old loyalties. Old fears. Family stories about love, safety, achievement, and silence. We began the work on ourselves, each of us, not to correct the other but to heal our own patterns. Therapy. Reflection. Honest inventory.

We did not outsource healing to the marriage. We brought our healing back to the marriage.

Communication became non-negotiable. Clear. Frequent. Specific. We stopped hinting and started naming. *I feel overwhelmed. I need help here. I am afraid of losing us.* We listened to understand rather than to win.

We created simple rituals that kept us connected:

- A weekly check-in with two questions only: *What are you carrying? How can I help?*
- An evening chat without phones.
- An early morning family walk to start the day fresh, energised and connected.

We wrote a clear vision we can say in one breath: *Healthy bodies. A simpler home. Work that serves. Time for the children and time for us. A marriage that values presence over performance.* We read it when decisions arise. Does this serve the vision? If the answer is No, we wait until the answer is clean. We allow no to stand when yes would cost us.

We changed how we lived the everyday. We agreed on a pace our bodies and calendars can keep. We stopped using achievements as proof of love. We stopped buying closeness with burnout. We put language around repair and gratitude: *I am sorry. I see what you carried. Here is what I can take today.* We rejected popular cynicism. We named the unseen labour. We traded tasks when it made sense, not to be even, but to be wise. We treated limits as information, not as failure.

By doing the work, we remembered why we chose each other in the first place. That remembering is the most reassuring and loving gesture we can offer one another.

We did not fix the marriage. We changed how we live inside it. We maintain capacity. We return to honest conversations before small problems become large ones. We notice what is beautiful and what is risky. We keep asking the question that reveals everything: *Who are we becoming?*

Alignment in Motherhood

The truth about motherhood, that loving my children fiercely and needing more to feel whole weren't contradictions, was one thing. And living them both required intentional structure.

I stopped apologising for having work I cared about. I stopped feeling guilty for needing time that was mine. But I also stopped letting work bleed into every margin, stealing presence from the people who needed me most.

I created clear boundaries:

- Work time was protected, but so was family time
- When I was with my children, I was fully with them: not half-present while mentally drafting emails
- When I was working or pursuing my own growth, I did it without guilt, knowing it made me a better mother, not a worse one.

I said NO to opportunities that would violate both. If it required me to sacrifice one for the other, the answer was NO, even when the opportunity looked impressive.

I built rituals that honoured both:

- **Mornings** belonged to my children before the workday began
- **Certain** evenings were sacred family time, no exceptions
- But I also claimed time for my work, my learning, my own becoming, and I stopped treating it as stolen time.

The alignment wasn't about perfect balance. It was about honest integration. Some seasons leaned more toward motherhood, others toward my work. But neither was abandoned. Both were honoured.

My children didn't need all of me, all the time. They needed the best of me, and that version only existed when I was whole, not diminished.

Key Moments

- Alignment feels less like a comeback and more like coming home to myself.

- My calendar tells the truth; when my time matches my values, life feels honest.

- Small shifts matter; earlier nights, clearer mornings, steadier days.

- My body responds to what I consume; I listen, adjust, and choose what serves me now.

- Alcohol did not serve my clarity; letting it go gave me my nights back.

- My mind also has a diet; quiet and careful curation protect my focus and spirit.

- I stopped curating other people's impressions and started honouring my reality.

- I stay where I feel most myself, and release what asks me to perform.

- Saying NO is care; it keeps my YES clear.

- Alignment is a daily practice of coherence: time, habits, consumption, and relationships moving in the same direction.

The Tree (that chose to thrive)

Pleasures in life: food, family and downtime

Public speaking and performance
(learning to own my story)

Teaching masterclasses around the world
(humbled and energised by teaching)

**Embracing freedom and wisdom,
in nature and solitude.**

**From perfection to freedom: owning
my story, on stage and in life**

Chapter 9

Growth

The Spring Beyond Childhood

After months of aligning my life with what I'd discovered—time, habits, relationships, marriage, motherhood, something unexpected began to stir.

Not another collapse. Not another reckoning. Something gentler. Something I hadn't felt in years: the quiet return of creative energy. Not the frantic kind that runs on adrenaline and approval, but something deeper. Steadier, and grounded.

I realised I was entering a new phase of life.

Call it midlife. Call it reinvention. Call it a return to truth. It felt seasonal rather than ceremonial. Spring again, but not the spring of childhood. A wiser spring. A second blooming.

This energy was different from what I'd known before. Not driven by performance or pressure, but by alignment. When your life finally reflects what you value, when your days match your truth, energy doesn't need to be forced. It rises naturally, like sap in a tree that's found its roots.

And with that energy came something I hadn't allowed myself in years: the desire to grow. Not to prove. Not to achieve. Simply to expand, explore, and be.

With that energy came curiosity, not the driven kind that chased credentials, but something gentler and more self-assured. A desire to explore what I'd never given myself permission to pursue. Not for achievement. Not for approval. But for allowing myself to be who I already am.

A Different Kind of Search

In this season of growth, I began searching for something entirely mine. Not another piece of excellence. Not another award. Something that would feed the part of me that had been starved while I was performing.

I realised that even during the years of achievement and busyness, a wiser part of me had been quietly unfulfilled, confused, and lonely, even. I was only just catching up to her.

I scanned my world with simple questions. What have I not considered? What might add richness, dimension, or meaning to this chapter? Not for a CV. Not for social proof. But for my soul.

The Wisdom School

In the months after aligning my life, I found a philosophy school. Modest. Volunteer-run. Non-religious. Politically neutral. It arrived when I was ready.

This was exactly what I had been searching for. Not a place to memorise Greek myths or recite creeds, but a space to explore practical philosophical insights that could shape how I lived—in my relationships, my work, my inner life. It drew from the wisdom of different cultures, historical events, languages, and religious teachings. All-encompassing. Heart-opening. And immediately useful.

It broadened my inner horizon and grounded me. It peeled me back and opened me up. It fed me simple, durable ideas. At that time I did not need a ladder to climb. I needed soil, roots, and stillness.

Virtues became the doorway. Courage. Wisdom. Justice. Moderation. They were not ideals to admire. They were tools. What does courage look like in a culture that worships comfort? What does wisdom sound like in a room that is always loud? What does justice mean when you finally stand for yourself?

Growth, for me, became less about expanding skill and more about deepening character.

Intentional Inputs

As I grew inwardly, I changed how I received the world. I became deliberate about what I allowed into my ears, mind and body.

For years I had absorbed noise by default. News humming in the background, half-listened conversations, content that left me more anxious than informed. It was not only information overload. It was energetic clutter.

As I grew, I could no longer tolerate what once filled the silence. I did not want filler. I wanted nourishment. I chose podcasts that lifted, videos that taught, and books that awakened. I stopped chasing what was trendy or popular and looked for what was true. I reclaimed authorship over how I related to reality. Not every voice needed entry. Not every urgency was mine to carry.

Claiming My Voice

For years my voice had been turned down. Not silenced, simply kept small. Shine, but safely. Be brilliant, but not too visible. Lead, but do not name it. I see now that this came from love and fear. Generational protection that had become a quiet prison.

My husband held up a mirror. "Do you realise that you are a leader without a title, Zen?" He noticed what I had ignored. People sought my thoughts. They mirrored my decisions. They trusted my discernment. The gravity was not loud, but it was real.

I let that in. My voice is not a threat. It is a tool, a bridge, and a gift. I chose to speak without performance. I chose to be imperfect in public. I went first. I learned what I had long denied myself because it felt too exposed. I shared skills, told stories, and offered lessons. Not from a pedestal, but from shared humanity.

Growing as a Mother

Growth arrived in the most intimate space of all. Motherhood.

It did not look like doing more. It looked like slowing down and softening. I realised I had felt lost because I was still trying to meet invisible expectations. I had assumed good mothering meant output and sacrifice. The truth was simpler. Presence is the work.

I listened to my children for who they are, not who I hoped they would become. We began real conversations. Fewer lectures. More questions. We asked what mattered to them and what lit them up. Guidance remained, with intention and care, and firmness when it was needed. We made sure we heard them before we redirected.

They are not my legacy or a second chance. They are their own people. My role is not to mould but to witness and honour.

Growing as a Daughter

As I softened into myself, I grew as a daughter. Old patterns and old stories did not vanish, but they loosened when I stopped trying to be the daughter they imagined and began relating as the woman I am.

I saw my parents as people. With their own fears and unfinished stories. Love was present even when it could not reach me in the way I needed. Growth here was quiet. Sometimes it was a softer reply. Sometimes it was a clean boundary. Sometimes it was the choice to listen without reaction.

Quiet Clarity

Change became visible. I showed up less rushed and more present. I listened with space. I spoke more plainly. I no longer needed to be everywhere or everything.

What mattered most was internal. My relationship with myself changed. I was living a life that felt like mine. I curated it around who I was becoming, not who I had been expected to be. I chose what stayed, what left, and what needed more room. Not out of defiance. But out of devotion.

This growth was not loud. It was felt. It settled into my nervous system. It changed the timbre of my voice. It shifted how I carried my body, how I entered a room and how I left one. I was not becoming a better version of myself. I was becoming myself.

The Full Circle

After all my careful self-work, I learned something simple: I do not grow alone. As I rose again, I sourced every useful resource. I realised I had the help I needed, and the help I did not know I needed.

When I think about growth done well, I think of Roger Federer. Not the highlights, but the team. Severin Lüthi beside the court for years. Pierre

Paganini building the engine for five sets and long seasons. A season with Tony Roche, later Ivan Ljubičić. Different eyes for different questions. No single guru. Clear roles. Humility to adjust.

That became my model. I keep a circle: a mentor for craft, a mentor for business, a guide for the inner work, and, when the knots are old, a therapist. Seasons change and mentors change with them. They do not fix me; they widen my view, name what I cannot yet see, and hold me to my word.

I choose as Federer chose. Values first. A clear brief. Consent for honesty. A cadence that keeps momentum. I use mentors actively: I send recordings and drafts, debrief the day a setback happens, and ask for patterns, not just tips. I do the homework and return with results.

I also let myself be witnessed. Courage grows faster when someone steady can see it—a coach who holds silence until the real answer arrives, an colleague who offers a better question, an elder who reminds me that excellence without presence is empty.

Sometimes the right move is to change the room. When the values shift, I thank the mentor, close the loop, and choose the next guide. That is not failure; it is respect for the work.

This is my full circle. I did the inner work, and I asked for help. Growth quickened. Drift stayed in check. The work became less lonely and more precise. Asking for help did not make me smaller. It made me real.

Key Moments

- Growth felt like a wiser spring, not a louder season.

- Virtues became tools, not slogans.

- I curate what enters my body and mind; not every urgency is mine to carry.

- My voice is a bridge. I can be imperfect and still be useful.

- In my family, I choose presence over performance and clean boundaries over noise.

Chapter 10

Expression

The first time I stepped back on stage after my collapse, it did not feel like a return. It felt like a rebirth.

In the months before, I had known darkness in its most intimate form. I folded into myself. Body curled. Spirit caved. Mind stripped bare. I learned what it meant to be brought to the fetal position, not just metaphorically, but also physically — the only posture that felt remotely safe when the world was too sharp and too loud.

From that position, life began again. Slowly at first. I found the strength to stand. I found the courage to look in the mirror and recognise myself. I found resources that fed me when I could not feed myself. Books, mentors, conversations, stillness. Then came movement. Tentative steps became a steady walk. A steady walk, in time, became flight.

When I felt ready to perform, I was sure the world had forgotten me. Surely colleagues had moved on. Surely the industry had erased my name. Surely audiences had shifted their gaze to newer stars.

I sent my résumé. I reached out to old contacts. I listened back to my recordings. On paper I met a woman I could barely believe was me. A globe-trotting pianist. A multilingual professional. A scholar and performer with world-class credentials. Had I really lived that life? Was it still in me?

The answer came quietly. Yes. Not from ego, but from memory and evidence. The world had not forgotten me. More importantly, I had stopped forgetting myself.

I reached out, still trembling. The warmth of the replies startled me. Invitations. Collaborations. Projects. A chorus of yes. The world I thought I had lost was still there, not only waiting but welcoming.

The difference this time was simple. I was not performing to prove. I was not standing under lights with perfection pressing on my shoulders. I was standing there with my whole self. Broken and recomposed. Scarred and renewed. The music no longer felt like a shield. It felt like an offering.

Returning to China

When an agent invited a colleague and me to tour China, to perform and teach across several cities, my first instinct was excitement. My second was fear. *What if I don't do a good job?*

Then a memory arrived, quiet but insistent. A memory that reminded me why I play at all.

I was a school girl in Perth, Australia, skipping down the street to my neighbour Zelda's house.

Zelda was a retired opera singer. She had warm eyes and a voice that still held the sheen of opera. She moved through the neighbourhood as if time did not own her, and she always had time for people. Zelda invited me to practise on her antique piano. After school I would arrive with sheet music and breathless stories. She hugged me, offered juice and biscuits, and settled into her chair. "So," she would beam, "what have you got for me today?"

I played everything from Joseph Haydn to Miriam Hyde, pouring in adolescent fire and the excitement of learning. I told her about competitions, concerts and the composers I loved. She listened as if every phrase mattered. Cheered me on, and told me how brilliant I was.

Years passed. I moved away and crossed continents. One day a parcel arrived. Inside was a letter from her daughter. Zelda had passed away. In her will she had spoken about a girl named Zen, who brought her music, joy, and hope, and asked that my recording of a Haydn Sonata to be played at her funeral.

I sat with the letter for a long time. Its tenderness and clarity settled in me. I could see Zelda smiling next to me. And I understood something I'd forgotten in all my years of chasing excellence: music was never meant to be a trophy. It was meant to be a gift. A bridge between hearts.

Excellence may have proved I could. But care, love, and connection would prove why I am here.

That memory, and that truth, became my compass for China. I wrote back and said yes. Not to prove I'd triumphed, but to connect with the people who I could serve.

Presence Over Perfection

I prepared thoroughly in technique and musicality, and just as carefully in stagecraft and the psychology of performance. I kept reminding myself that my purpose was not to prove brilliance or parade a transformation. My purpose was to be myself, to share what I had learned, and to connect.

The nerves still came. I asked the old questions. *Am I up to it? Am I ready?* In the space that opened, I met the younger part of me who wanted calm and perspective. I could offer those now. I could parent myself with compassion. The world does not need another genius. It needs open hearts and listening ears. Audiences do not need perfection. They need presence.

Travel days felt familiar, yet my heart was prepared differently. Logistics remained the same. Sound checks. Lighting. Rehearsal notes. They no longer felt like pressure points to control. They felt like gentle preparations for connection. I walked the streets in the evenings and let the city speak. I was not rushing. I was receiving.

The night before my first major performance, I stood in a hotel room, performance frocks hanging by the mirror, shoes lined by the wall, the city pulsing below. For a moment I asked, *is my life back on track?*

The answer was NO. My life had taken on a new path. A path of my choice, and my calling. I did not need to be impeccable. I needed to be me.

When the concert days arrived, I poured my whole self into the music. I played for meaning as much as for beauty or accuracy. What the music meant to me. What it meant to the composer. What it might mean to us now. I spoke to the audience from the heart, without a script. I drew the story and life wisdom out of every composition, every phrase, and every emotion. I wanted to offer something that could make a day lighter, a life more hopeful, and a world more meaningful.

As I was driven through the city to the hall, I checked in with myself. Light. Ready. Willing to surrender. Applause rose as I walked on. I felt grounded and gracious. I felt bare.

The lights faded, the applause dissolved, and silence invited me to begin. I realised that the girl in my old recordings was still me. The years of work, the teachers, the goals and the questions. My skills were present. My mind, body, and spirit were aligned. I placed my hands on the keys and noticed I was not shaking. My breath was steady. I could feel the audience with me.

Mozart unfolded. It was about him. His losses and his strange mix of grace and ache. I sobbed with his lines and sighed with his phrases. I felt the audience breathing with me. The loudest emotions lived in the stillness between notes. It was simple and it was profound.

City after city, the response confirmed what I felt on stage. The connection was genuine. The impact was real. When the tour ended, the invitations returned without hesitation. People thanked me not because they had never seen excellence. They had. They thanked me because they felt heard and served. They remembered why they loved music. They remembered that music is not a contest of mastery. It is a communion of meaning.

Expression, I understood, is not about impressing. It is about connecting. It is about living to serve.

The Courage to Express in Life

Expression did not stop at the piano. It reshaped how I spoke and how I related. The courage I found on stage began to appear in conversations and choices.

I learned to be honest and empathetic at the same time. I stopped suppressing my opinions or hiding my needs. I began to voice them clearly and with care. I stood in truth without losing love.

This also changed how I taught. I no longer preach excellence. I teach presence, awareness, self-compassion, curiosity, and attuned learning. I do not hide behind perfect plans. I let students see my process and my questions. I say *I do not know* when I do not. I share my mistakes and what they taught me. We notice what sparks them. We ask how the learning serves their real lives. I pay close attention to their habits and the challenges they carry. The standards stay high, held with kindness. Authority does not shrink. Trust deepens.

I stopped paddling to keep everyone pleased. I stopped prioritising plans that would please everyone. Even when I had to make hard calls, I reminded myself that my decisions were thoughtful and grounded in service. With that, the weight of pleasing fell away. I felt free.

Whether on stage before thousands or in a quiet conversation with one person, the principle stayed the same. Authentic expression is not about being perfect. It is about being present. It is not about having all the answers. It is about showing up with a whole heart. It is not about impressing. It is about connecting.

Expression, I learned, is how we move from becoming to being. It is the bridge between inner transformation and outer impact. When we express from truth rather than performance, from presence rather than perfection, we give others permission to do the same.

And in that exchange, something sacred happens: we remember why we are here.

Key Moments

On stage

- I perform to connect, not to prove.

- Presence over perfection is my anchor. I prepare, then I let go.

- I approve myself first, and the audience feels that ease.

- Before I walk on, I set a simple intention: serve, not display.

- I trust silence. The pauses carry feelings.

- I hold a person in mind, not a crowd. The work is people.

In life

- Authentic expression, for me, is truth with care.

- I say what matters with respect and clarity.

- I measure success by resonance, not applause.

- When nerves rise, I offer calm to my younger self.

In teaching

- I no longer preach excellence. I teach presence, awareness, self-compassion, curiosity and attuned learning.

- I let students see my process and my questions.

- I keep standards high and hold them with kindness. Trust deepens.

My practices

- Before a performance or hard conversation, I write one line of intention. Who am I serving?

- I take two breaths and scan my body for ease and bracing.

- Afterward I ask one question. Did this connect?

Chapter 11

Body, Mind and Spirit

Expression had taught me to show up fully—on stage, in teaching, in relationships. But showing up fully required something I was still learning: the integration of body, mind, and spirit.

I had always been a spiritual person. Even as a child, I felt drawn to something larger than myself, energised by connection and meaning. But somewhere along the way, I learned to let my mind rule everything. My intellect became the driver, my body the vehicle, and my spirit, though still flickering, was relegated to the background, acknowledged only when convenient.

For years, I lived as if thinking harder, planning better, and willing stronger would solve everything. My mind was brilliant, capable, relentless. But it had also become a tyrant, overriding my body's signals and silencing my spirit's whispers.

My collapse had revealed a different truth: I was not just a mind piloting a body. I was all three: body, mind, and spirit, interdependent and inseparable.

Understanding that was one thing. Living it was another.

Body

It was a confronting discovery. My body was as powerful, as wise, and as vulnerable as my mind. For years I believed my success came in spite of a small frame and because of sheer will. The body was the vehicle, the mind the driver. That was my story.

Then I encountered a line that stopped me cold: *the body keeps the score.* I began to see what I had ignored. My body was not passive. It had been witnessing everything, storing what I would not process, holding truths my mind refused to name.

When life became unbearable and my thoughts tangled, it was my body that screamed for help. Exhaustion, colds, rashes, relentless fatigue. Not random inconveniences, but alarms. At rock bottom, my coping mechanisms collapsed and my body took over. It refused to continue on the same path when my mind could not.

So I listened. I gave the body agency. Not with quick fixes or treats, but with real attention. I stopped jolting myself awake with caffeine and hiding symptoms with creams. I built daily, sustainable care. I noticed. I rested. I let the body recover.

What I found was simple and shocking. My body was tired. Silenced for too long. It did not have to stay that way. Now I check in often. *How does this feel? Where is there ease? Where is there bracing?* Over time the relationship changed. My body is no longer a servant I drive to collapse. It is a friend, a mentor, a partner.

Mind

If the body forced me to listen, the mind reminded me who I had always been. I am a thinker, a believer and a doer. I grew up praised for a sharp mind. I wore those words as identity. My mind became my engine and my shield. For a long time it carried me far.

There was a shadow side. The same force that drove me could also trap me. Overthinking. Perfectionism. What-ifs and not-enoughs. My mind demanded more when my body had nothing left. It called rest weakness and told me to keep going. I obeyed, until I could not.

I did not discard my mind. I redefined its role. It was never meant to be a dictator. It is a questioner, a seeker, a maker of meaning. Now I watch it with kindness. I notice the stories it spins and the fears it inflates. I do not silence those thoughts, and I do not mistake them for truth. I ask my body how those thoughts land. Do they tighten or expand me? Do they align with my values?

In this partnership, my mind is luminous again. Curious, creative, clear. When it works with the wisdom of the body and the grounding of spirit, it serves rather than rules.

Spirit

The idea of spirit was never foreign to me. Even as a child I felt drawn to something larger, energising and steadying at once. I avoided the word for years because it sounded vague to some, or too religious to others. Now I have no hesitation. Spirit is what lifted me when the body and mind had nothing left. Spirit reminded me that life is more than survival or performance.

Spirit feels like a flame. It brightens when tended and dims when neglected. It is not static. It needs care. Some days it burns high, some days it is a quiet glow. Even then, it never disappears. It waits to be fed.

I once heard a monk say that mastery is not about never getting distracted, it is about getting good at returning to what matters. That is my practice now. Not eliminating imbalance, but returning. I return through music, stillness, community, and service. I feed the flame with what brings awe and meaning. I protect it with rest, reflection, and clear boundaries. I share it, because spirit grows when it is lifted.

When body, mind, and spirit are in conversation, I feel whole. My body grounds me. My mind questions and creates. My spirit reminds me why it matters. When I face a decision, I consult all three. *How does it feel? What do I see? What serves?* It takes seconds. It keeps me honest.

These days I walk into rooms differently. Not louder. Not flashier. But whole. I do not rehearse my value in my head. I arrive with presence. People often comment. They are not responding to performance. They are responding to coherence. Words and values that match. Authority and softness, each when needed. We all feel misalignment. We also feel alignment when it is real. It is magnetic not because it is powerful, but because it is authentic.

Key Moments

Body

- My body is not a vehicle for my mind. It is a witness and a teacher.

- Symptoms are messages. Fatigue, tension, and flare-ups are alarms, not annoyances.

- Daily care beats occasional rescue. Rest, nourishment, sunlight, movement and gentleness.

- I ask often: where is there ease, where am I bracing? Then I adjust.

Mind

- My mind is brilliant, and it is not the boss.

- I notice the story and do not marry it. I observe, then check how it lands in my body.

- Curiosity is stronger than control. I ask what is true, what is useful, what is kind.

- I choose discernment over perfection. Clear beats clever.

Spirit

- My spirit is a flame. It brightens when tended and dims when ignored.

- I feed it with awe, music, stillness, service and good company.

- Returning is the practice. When I drift, I come back. No drama, just return.

My practices

- One minute body check each morning. I name one place of ease and one place of strain.

- One thought audit daily. Is this true? Is it helpful? Can I soften it?

- One act to feed the spirit. A page of music, a quiet walk, a simple kindness.

- Before decisions I consult all three. How does it feel? What do I see? Who do I serve?

Chapter 12

Crescendo: A Life Beyond the Spotlight

Body, mind, and spirit, once fragmented, now in conversation. That integration changed everything. It gave me the foundation I'd been missing: not just knowing what mattered, but feeling it in my bones, thinking it through with clarity, and sensing it in my soul.

From that wholeness, I could finally see where I'd been and where I was going. Not with a rigid plan, but with guiding principles. A compass rather than a map.

This is what those principles look like.

These days, I still pursue excellence, but I've redefined what excellence means. My effort is no longer fueled by competition or the need to prove. Instead, it is a daily practice of returning to myself. To the person I am. To the person I want to be. To the person I am destined to be.

Some of the stories that inspire me most are not about triumph, but about failure, especially from people who seem, from the outside, to have done nothing but win.

"I have failed over and over and over again in my life. And that is why I succeed." **– Michael Jordan**

"Life is bigger than any single match or moment." **– Roger Federer**

Michael Jordan's career included more than 10,000 missed shots, nearly 300 losses, and 26 failed game-winning attempts. It's hard to reconcile those numbers with the image of the ultimate champion, the man who defined basketball excellence for an entire generation. But that's what makes his words powerful: success is not the absence of failure; it is built on it.

Roger Federer, in his graduation address at Dartmouth College, spoke of failure as an inevitable part of progress. The people who keep moving forward are not those who never falter, but those who learn how to respond when they do. And he reminded his audience that life is bigger than any single match or moment, a truth that, once grasped, frees us from letting one setback define us.

These lessons echo deeply with what I have lived. For so long, I pushed myself to avoid failure at all costs, rehearsing harder, polishing every detail, perfecting every move. But that pursuit was exhausting and fragile. The moment something didn't go to plan, it felt like my worth was at risk.

Now, I see it differently. Failure is not a verdict; it is a teacher. It's an invitation to return to my values, to my body, to the person I want to be. And in that return, I have found something more enduring than perfection: the ability to keep showing up, even after the miss.

"Water can flow, or it can crash. Be water, my friend." – Bruce Lee

Water has always fascinated me. It is soft and yielding, yet it carves valleys through stone. It adapts to any container, yet it cannot be contained for long. It sustains life, yet it can also reshape it entirely.

For much of my life, I built myself like a fortress: structured, disciplined, and precise. That strength carried me far, but it also made me rigid. I sought like-minded people who shared my purpose and drive, but I also longed for a space where I could set the armour down, where I could rest and simply be.

Bruce Lee's words remind me that real strength lies not only in holding form, but in knowing when to flow: to adapt without losing my essence, to receive without resistance, to let life move me without being swept away.

In my pursuit of freedom from perfection, I've learned that water's power is in its balance: direction with ease, movement with presence, force with grace. This is how I now try to live, with a purpose to pursue, a community to belong to, and the courage to surrender to the current when it's time to let go.

"Your children are not your children…"
– Kahlil Gibran

"Your children are not your children. They are the sons and daughters of Life's longing for itself. They come through you but not from you, And though they are with you, yet they belong not to you. You may give them your love but not your thoughts, For they have their own thoughts. You may house their bodies but not their souls, For their souls dwell in the house of tomorrow, which you cannot visit, not even in your dreams. You may strive to be like them, but seek not to make them like you. For life goes not backward nor tarries with yesterday. You are the bows from which your children as living arrows are sent forth." – Kahlil Gibran

I have always adored this poem, not just for its beauty, but for the beacon of light it offers. It holds a fine, almost surgical precision in the way it invites us to examine and question what we believe we "possess" in life. I loved it and related to it long before I became a mother. Even in the years when I thought I would never be a mother, these words spoke to me.

Perhaps it was because, as a child, I felt liberated by the love, freedom, and grace within this poem. It reminded me that love is not ownership, that guidance is not control, and that the greatest gift we can offer is space for another soul to grow into itself.

These days, I am learning to live that truth with my own children. I am learning to listen deeply, to hear not only their words, but the person they are becoming beneath those words. I am learning to have the courage to release the expectations I once carried, the ones I inherited, and the ones I thought I needed to uphold. I am learning to truly appreciate the wholeness they were born with.

I now see that my role is not to give them wholeness, mould them into shape, or discipline them into my vision, but to facilitate, to inspire, and to role-model. To be the steady bow from which they can launch, not in the direction I choose, but toward the horizon that calls them.

"Nobody is going to come along one day and convince you that you're enough."
– Brianna Wiest

One idea that stayed with me during my recovery, as I rebuilt my mental strength and rewrote my inner narratives, was this: nobody is going to come along one day and convince you that you're enough. That work is yours.

I thought about it constantly. I would play those words in my head while driving to a business meeting, before stepping into the spotlight, and in the quiet moments of reflecting on the day. I began to share it with my students, and with anyone who needed to hear it. Because it's true: waiting for the world to crown you "enough" is a game with no end. At some point, you have to decide to claim it for yourself.

After years of soul searching and hard-earned lessons, I realised something liberating: I do not need credentials for everything I do or every role I embody. I am unique as I am, and I am as powerful, useful, and worthy as I am. My audience is not everyone; it never was meant to be. I simply need to show up and share in service of those who are ready for what I offer, who need my presence and my gifts.

It is time to stop procrastinating, reinventing myself endlessly, constantly upskilling in search of some phantom readiness. I am ready now. The mountain I have been so desperately trying to climb is, and has always been, me.

Love, Hope, and Authentic Power

I've come to see that, in our own ways, we are all searching for a few common things: love, hope, and power. Love: to feel seen, valued, and connected. Hope: to believe in a future that is worth moving toward. And power: to know we have agency over our lives and the ability to influence the world around us.

But the kind of power we pursue matters. Gary Zukav, speaking on Oprah's show, explained it this way: "External power comes and goes, authentic power you never lose. Until you develop authentic power, you'll continue to create painful experiences in your life. You are living a life of authentic power. It means to be excited about what you are doing, to be fulfilled and be fulfilling. You forget to be angry, frightened, you know you are on this earth to do something, to give gifts, that you are doing that something to give those gifts, you are fully engaged to be in the present moment."

External power comes from the outside, from wealth, titles, recognition, influence over others. It can be intoxicating, but it's unstable, because it depends on things we can't fully control. When we haven't developed authentic power, we grasp for the external kind to feel relevant, safe, or worthy.

Authentic power is different. It's born when our personality serves the calling of our soul, when we live on purpose, in service, and in alignment with our deepest values. It doesn't need to be defended or performed. It doesn't rely on applause or permission. It's quiet but unshakeable.

When I first heard Zukav speak about this, it struck me how many of my own struggles, and the struggles I've seen in others, come from confusing these two kinds of power. We chase the external version because it's visible, measurable, and rewarded. But without the internal version, the pursuit becomes endless, and the wins feel strangely hollow.

Today, I know that love, hope, and authentic power are cultivated from within, then expressed outward. And when they are aligned, life becomes less about proving, and more about living in a way that feels authentic.

The Sacred Work of Teaching

This understanding has transformed how I approach my work. When that woman at the park years ago suggested I should be "doing what I'm meant to do," she couldn't have known that I already was.

Teaching, or rather, guiding, coaching, facilitating, isn't what I settled for. It's where everything I've learned converges: the musical discipline, the interpreter's training, the mother's wisdom, the performer's presence, the woman's understanding of what authentic living costs.

I create spaces where people can remember who they are and what they're here for. I help them name the real problem under the surface and find their way back to clarity and power. It's humbling. Sacred. And my heart is all the way in.

From Freedom Back to Perfection, with Love

And now, we circle back to the Zen who had the near-miss car accident. I see her clearly, frozen for a moment on that stretch of road, her pulse racing, her mind stunned into silence. She is still wearing the armour of perfection then, still carrying the weight of performance, still believing her worth depends on how well she plays the part.

If I could sit beside her now, I would place a hand on her shoulder and tell her: You don't have to do it all. You don't have to prove anything. The applause will fade, the roles will change, but your value is not tied to either.

I would tell her that the exhaustion she feels is not a flaw; it is a signal. A signal to pause, to listen, to return to herself. I would tell her that one day, she will no longer measure her life in achievements or failures, but in moments of presence, in choices that align with her values, in relationships that nourish rather than drain.

I would tell her to take care of her body, to trust its cues. To embrace failure as a teacher. To protect her energy as fiercely as she once pursued success. And above all, I would tell her that she is already enough, not because of what she has done, but because of who she already is.

She would not believe all of it in that moment. But I would smile and let her know that she doesn't have to. One day, she will live it.

And so we close this chapter and this book with the same woman we began with. But she is no longer rushing through life on autopilot. She is here, now. Living not to impress, but to express. Not to climb endlessly, but to stand grounded in her own light. This is her crescendo.

"In music and in life, it is the pauses that allow the heart to catch up, the meaning to land, and the connection to be made. Without pauses, everything blurs. With them, both music and life find their shape." – Zen Zeng

As a musician trained for the world's great concert halls, I have always known the importance of allowing silence between musical ideas. To let the sound of the previous phrase dissipate, to give the hall's acoustics time to absorb the resonance, to allow the audience space to feel what has just been expressed before the next idea begins. Without that silence, the music becomes crowded. With it, each note has meaning.

I realise now that life asks for the same discipline. For years, I ran from task A to B to C to D without pause, believing that endurance was the mark of strength. But it wasn't the pressure or the workload that undid me; it was the lack of space in between.

Today, I know that rest between tasks is not indulgence. It is the silence between the notes. It is what allows clarity to rise, emotions to settle, and the next action to land with precision and purpose. Just as in music, it is the pause that gives life its shape.

Surrender and Beyond Crescendo

But wisdom isn't just philosophical; it's practical. And life has a way of testing us when we least expect it.

As I reached a deep sense of freedom, clarity, and grounded excitement about my life and my pursuit, I also knew that life is ever evolving. Each season brings its own tests, each choice another chance to adjust and evolve.

One evening, I felt such a test arrive. It was a weekday, the kind of night when the house finally grew quiet, and I was catching my breath between the demands of work and home. My phone buzzed with a message. It was from an old colleague, an extraordinary musician I admire, respect, and with whom I enjoy working.

He suggested a new project, a musical collaboration with another extraordinary artist. The three of us, he wrote, could create something powerful: show-stopping, unforgettable. He told me that I was the one and only pianist they wanted. They could not think of anyone else more skilled, aligned, and exciting to work with.

I read the message once. Twice. A third time. My heart leaped, first with delight, then with pride, then with the old spark of anticipation. What an honour, I thought. What a career-defining opportunity. For a moment, I could already see the posters, hear the applause, and feel the familiar rhythm of prestige and performance taking hold.

But then, something else stirred. Not my body pacing with doubt this time, but a quieter presence: the little voice inside me, or perhaps the imaginary elder who often appears in my mind's eye. They did not speak, but simply gazed at me with that steady, wise look. As if to say: Pause. Listen. Is this truly yours?

So I did the one thing the old version of me never would have done: I waited. I put the phone down. I gave the silence its space, like between two musical ideas, letting the echo of the invitation dissipate. I let my inner wisdom rise to meet me.

I stepped outside and noticed the air, cool and fresh against my skin. I listened to the faint web of sounds around me, let colours and shapes fill my eyes, felt the weight of my sleeves against my arms, the gentle release of my jaw. For the first time in a long while, I let my senses, not my ambition, be the guide.

The next day, the inner noise grew loud. What if I decline and the chance never comes again? What if I offend them? What if this is the opportunity that would finally prove me? The old reflex to perform, to please, pressed hard. But then another thought came, steadier, truer: My music, my time, my energy are no longer about building prestige.

They are for service, for people, for the work I am called to do now.

After days of this back-and-forth, the answer arrived. Not loud, but steady. Not dramatic, but undeniable.

Yes, what an honour. But no. Not for me. Not now. Not anymore.

The moment I made the decision, something inside me shifted. It was as if a weight I didn't know I was carrying finally dropped. My body felt settled, my chest opened, and I smiled without effort. I felt both grounded and light, as though I had stepped into a new spaciousness within myself.

That was the moment I realised: I am still evolving, but now I evolve with clarity, alignment, and purpose as my anchors. My voice, once buried beneath performance and expectation, now speaks with clarity, humility, and truth, even when it means saying no to extraordinary opportunities. My alignment keeps me rooted in what matters most, choosing rest over productivity when my body asks for it, guiding my choices so they remain consistent with my values. And my purpose gives me direction, not as a rigid map, but as a compass that allows me to teach from experience rather than theory, to navigate with both confidence and openness.

These anchors don't stop the waves from coming, but they keep me steady when they do. They allow me to grow without losing myself, to change without abandoning what is essential, and to keep moving forward even when the path ahead is uncertain.

And in that moment, I thought of her, the Zen from years ago, sitting in her car after the near-miss accident, numb and frightened, wondering if she could keep up the performance. I look back at her now with love, with empathy, with gratitude. She was so desperate to prove, to hold it all together. But she didn't know then what I know now:

That freedom comes not from seizing every opportunity, but from choosing with intention.

That power is not in proving, but in aligning. That clarity is not forced, but received in the pauses.

If I could whisper to her, I would say: Be patient, my friend. The life you are striving so hard to control will one day soften. The voice you think you've lost will return, steady and true. And when it does, you will know how to say yes with joy, and how to say no with peace. You will not be defined by what you achieve, but by how aligned you are when you choose.

This, to me, is what living in crescendo truly means.

This Is Your Crescendo

You've walked this journey with me through the collapse of a perfectly constructed life, through the silence that followed, through the uncomfortable truth-telling and the gradual alignment with what matters most. You've witnessed the growth that comes not from striving, but from listening. You've seen what happens when we stop performing and start expressing.

Now it's time to discover your own voice, alignment, and purpose.

Your crescendo will not look like mine. It's not meant to. It will carry your rhythm, your truth, your unique expression. But it will ask of you what it asked of me: to stop rehearsing the life you think you should live and step fully into the one that is already yours.

The S.T.A.G.E. framework you've learned isn't just theory; it's a practice. **Stillness** isn't just the absence of noise; it's the presence of listening. **Truth** isn't just honesty; it's the courage to live authentically. **Alignment** isn't just balance; it's the integration of values with action. **Growth** isn't just progress; it's the wisdom to evolve without losing yourself. **Expression** isn't just performance; it is about showing up as who you truly are.

Start today with one pause. Before your next meeting, before responding to that email, before saying yes to another obligation, pause. Give yourself the space between the notes. Ask yourself:

Is this truly mine? Listen for the answer that comes not from your mind's should, but from your body's knowing.

Return to yourself. Anchor in what matters. Choose the relationships, the work, the moments that light you from within. Let go of what drains you. Give your gifts freely. Live in a way that is both deeply present and fiercely alive.

Because the music of your life is already swelling. The world is waiting for you to play it as only you can.

This is your crescendo.

Key Moments

- Excellence now means coming home to who I am.

- Failure builds the muscle to success.

- Water wisdom: hold form, and know when to flow.

- Love without ownership; guide with open hands.

- "Enough" is an inside job — I claim it.

- Seek authentic power, not performative status.

- My work is presence and guidance, not performance.

- The pauses give life shape; alignment makes every choice clean.

Acknowledgement

The village it takes to write a book, is the same
village it takes to lead a life of authenticity and
abundance. To those who instilled the pursuit of
excellence—your lessons became the foundation
I rebuilt upon. I am grateful beyond measure.

Appendix

S.T.A.G.E. Framework: Practical Applications

STILLNESS: Creating Space to Listen

The Body Check-In Practice *(inspired by Chapter 11)*

- Before major decisions, pause and ask: "How does this land in my body?"
- Notice: Does it expand or contract you? Energise or drain?
- Practise the "5-breath pause" between commitments

The Marie-Zen Question *(inspired by Chapter 6)*

- Hold each obligation, relationship, commitment and ask: "Does this still spark joy?"

- If not: "What did this teach me?" Then release with gratitude.

Reflection Questions:

- *When did I last feel truly rested (not just physically)?*
- *What am I carrying that isn't mine to carry?*
- *If I had no audience, what would I choose?*

TRUTH: Facing What Is

The Time Audit *(inspired by Chapter 8)*

- Track how you spend time for one week
- Compare to your stated values/priorities
- Ask: "What does my calendar say I actually value?"

The Relationship Review *(inspired by Chapters 6-7)*

- List your key relationships
- Mark: Energising (+), Draining (-), or Neutral (0)
- Ask: "Who am I performing for vs. who sees the real me?"

Reflection Questions:

- *What story am I telling myself that's no longer true?*
- *Where am I seeking external validation instead of internal knowing?*
- *What would I pursue if no one was watching?*

ALIGNMENT: Living Your Values

The Daily Rhythm Experiment *(inspired by Chapter 8)*

- Try **one** change for 7 days (earlier bedtime, morning routine, saying no to one thing daily)
- **Notice:** energy levels, mood, clarity
- **Keep** what serves, release what doesn't

The Boundary Practice

- **Identify** one area where you consistently over-give
- **Practise:** "Let me think about that and get back to you"
- **Notice** the difference between guilt (old pattern) and relief (alignment)

Reflection Questions:

- *Am I the CEO of my own life or just middle management?*
- *What would change if I trusted my body's wisdom?*
- *Where am I saying yes when I mean no?*

GROWTH: Evolving Without Losing Yourself

The Failure Reframe *(inspired by Chapter 12)*

- List 3 recent "failures" or disappointments
- For each ask: "What did this teach me about who I'm becoming?"
- Practise: "I'm learning..." instead of "I failed..."

The Voice Reclaiming Exercise *(inspired by Chapter 9)*

- Complete: "If I could speak without fear of judgment, I would say..."
- Start small: share one authentic opinion per day
- Notice: Who celebrates your voice vs. who wants you smaller?

Reflection Questions:

- *What am I ready to outgrow?*
- *How can I honour both who I've been and who I'm becoming?*
- *What gifts am I withholding from the world?*

EXPRESSION: Showing Up Authentically

The Service Question *(inspired by Chapter 12)*

- Before saying yes to opportunities, ask: "Does this serve my authentic purpose?"
- Practise saying: "That sounds wonderful, but it's not aligned with my current direction"

The Creative Expression Practice

- Choose one form of expression just for you (not performance, not perfection)
- 15 minutes daily: write, move, create without agenda
- Notice what wants to emerge when no one's watching

Reflection Questions:

- *How do I want to be remembered?*
- *What would I create if I couldn't fail?*
- *Who benefits when I show up as my full self?*

Recommended Reading

These works have accompanied me through moments of reflection, challenge, and renewal — offering language for what was once only felt, and reminding me that growth is both an inner and shared art.

Viktor E. Frankl — *Man's Search for Meaning*
A timeless reminder that freedom begins in the space between stimulus and response.

Eckhart Tolle — *The Power of Now*
A guide to presence — quiet, piercing, and transformative.

Brianna Wiest — *The Mountain Is You*
A modern reflection on self-sabotage, healing, and inner evolution.

Joseph Deitch — *Elevate: An Essential Guide to Life*
An invitation to grow through awareness, curiosity, and conscious action.

Gary Zukav — *The Seat of the Soul*

A profound exploration of authenticity, intention, and the evolution of the spirit.

Alain de Botton — *The Architecture of Happiness*
A lyrical meditation on how our surroundings shape the lives we aspire to build.

May these books meet you where you are — and accompany you, as they did me, toward clarity, courage, and freedom.

Beyond Crescendo

The Crescendo Circle

Are you craving more clarity — not just in thought, but in how you live and lead?

Do you want to stay connected to your purpose, even when the tempo of life accelerates?

Are you ready to turn insight into action — and sustain growth with rhythm and accountability?

Welcome to *The Crescendo Circle.*

I founded this private community for mindful-achievers, leaders, founders and creatives, who are ready to grow with intention.

Here, reflection meets structure. Together we build systems, habits, and conversations that help you grow and keep you aligned — personally, professionally, and creatively.

Each season, we explore guided themes from *The Crescendo Method:* combining music, mindset, and evidence-based frameworks in a supportive and accountable environment.

Members take part in **Pause & Play** sessions — immersive experiences blending live piano and guided reflection, and engage with **guest speakers** who bring fresh insight from diverse fields of leadership, education, science, and the arts.

Our members don't just seek balance; we practise it, together.

Join us for live sessions, reflection labs, and in-person events designed to turn awareness into alignment.

Visit www.zenzeng.net to learn more or register for the waitlist.

Your next movement begins here.

About the Author

Z en Zeng (PhD) is a concert pianist, conference interpreter, professional speaker and teacher. Her career bridges music, performance psychology, diplomacy, education and leadership. With performances and collaborations across four continents, she is known for her rare blend of artistry, intellect, and cross-cultural insight.

Zen is the found of **Crescendo with Zen,** a practice that integrates music, mindset, and performance psychology to help thoughtful-achievers and organisations align excellence with presence. Through her talks, coaching, and immersive experiences, including *Pause & Play* and *The Crescendo Circle* — Zen distils the mindset and methods of elite performance into actionable tools for living and leading with clarity, composure, and purpose.

Zen lives in Melbourne with her three pianos, two kids, and the one and only husband.

Learn more and stay connected at www.zenzeng.net

Zen Zeng (PhD)

Keynote performer | High-Performance Mentor |
Concert Pianist | Conference Interpreter |
Author | Founder of Crescendo Circle

Helping thoughtful achievers strive for excellence
with presence, clarity and alignment.

Signature Keynotes & Frameworks

After experiencing the cost of unsustainable excellence firsthand, Zen developed
two frameworks that are transforming how leaders and teams approach
communication and performance.

T.U.N.E.™ — teaches Deep Listening as a critical leadership skill that strengthens
connection, sharpens decision-making, and elevates team performance.

S.T.A.G.E.™ — guides teams and individuals from perfection-driven burnout to
sustainable, aligned excellence.

About Zen

Zen's career bridges **music, psychology, diplomacy, education, and leadership**,
bringing a rare harmony of artistry and intellect to every stage.

Having performed on four continents and interpreted in high-pressure diplomatic,
legal, and commercial settings, Zen translates her **global** experience into **practical**
frameworks for sustainable excellence and authentic leadership.

She is the **founder of The Crescendo Circle** — a global community for high achievers
learning to lead with presence, beyond performance.

Maestro of Deep Listening
Transform how you perform, connect and thrive.

Based in:
Melbourne, Australia,
available globally.

Why Book Zen

- A **world-class concert pianist** who performs as she speaks — creating unforgettable multi-sensory keynotes.
- A **conference interpreter** skilled at precision, empathy, and nuance in high-stakes environments.
- A **high-performance mentor** who translates mastery into mindset and wellbeing.
- A **master teacher and facilitator** who makes complex ideas actionable, relatable, and deeply human.
- A **storyteller with wit and warmth**, bridging intellect and intuition to help audiences rediscover their inner rhythm.

Speaking Topics

1. **The Hidden Power of Deep Listening™** — How to elevate performance, relationships, and leadership through presence.
2. **From Perfection to Freedom** — Redefining success and sustaining excellence without burnout.
3. **The Art of Performing Under Pressure** — Lessons from the concert stage for business and leadership.
4. **Lead with Presence, Beyond Performance** — Transform how you communicate, connect, and inspire lasting impact.

Testimonials:

Prof. Paul Kelly – Chief Medical Office of Australia (2020-24)
"Zen has a unique ability to connect people and ideas across disciplines and cultures. She brings insight, humanity, and precision to everything she does."

Joanna Zhou – Audit Senior Manager
"Zen is authentic and candid on stage... I drew so much energy from her stories and messages, feeling she was speaking right to me. You will be amazed."

Michelle Jennison – Teacher
"Zen is pure presence, authenticity and honesty. Be prepared to grow your mind, expand your awareness, be held accountable and be inspired to positive action."

Testimonials

Prof. Paul Kelly – Chief Medical Officer of Australia (2020-24)

Zen has a unique ability to connect people and ideas across disciplines and cultures. She brings insight, humanity, and precision to everything she does: a rare combination that makes her stand out in every field she enters.

Jessica Gethin - Australian conductor

Zen is an artist of remarkable sensitivity, integrity and imagination. Her unwavering commitment to excellence and her ability to connect deeply through music and collaboration are truly inspiring. With creative vision and quiet leadership, she brings depth, generosity and artistry to everything she does – and in her writing, she extends that same creative spirit and authenticity beyond the concert platform, sharing her artistry and insight in a new and meaningful way.

Martin Dougall - Global Head and Senior Partner, KPMG

Zen speaks from the heart of a concert pianist, the mind of a philosopher, and the soul of an authentic traveller. Steeped in the lessons of experience and expertise, Zen personifies deep thinking, weaving together the lessons of music, metaphor and meaning in ways that challenge and inspire.

Dr. Jonathan Shock – Director of AI Initiative at the University of Cape Town

Zen doesn't just perform art, she lives its impact. I've known her for nearly two decades and each encounter leaves me struck by the same qualities: presence, depth, and connection. Zen is both intuitive and analytical, driven yet deeply caring. She has that rare gift of turning art into a bridge between people, ideas, and worlds.

Joanna Zhou – Audit Senior Manager

Zen is authentic and candid on stage, which easily drew me to the context of the music and made me feel connected to the piece. She's an all-rounder: an excellent teacher, a trustworthy friend, loving mother, an amazing musician, a deep thinker. I think people will draw energy from her and get inspired. You will be amazed.

Michelle Jennison – friend

Zen is pure presence, authenticity and honesty. She cares deeply about people and brings curiosity, depth and kindness to every conversation. Be prepared to grow your mind, expand your awareness, be held accountable and be inspired to positive action.

Notes

Notes

9 781923 583528